# Business Communications, the Real World, and Your Career

James A. Seguin

OUACHITA TECHNICAL COLLEGE

**South-Western College Publishing**
Thomson Learning℠

Australia • Canada • Denmark • Japan • Mexico • New Zealand • Philippines
Puerto Rico • Singapore • South Africa • Spain • United Kingdom • United States

*Business Communication, the Real World, and Your Career* by James A. Seguin

Publisher: Dave Shaut
Acquisitions Editor: Pamela M. Person
Marketing Manager: Sarah J. Woelfel
Production Editor: Sandra Gangelhoff
Manufacturing Coordinator: Dana Began Schwartz
Cover Designer: Jennifer Martin-Lambert
Cover Illustration: Nikolai Punin / Stock Illustration Source
Printer: Webcom

Printed in Canada
1 2 3 4 5 02 01 00 99

For more information contact South-Western College Publishing, 5101 Madison Road, Cincinnati, Ohio, 45227 or find us on the Internet at http://www.swcollege.com

**For permission to use material from this text or product, contact us by**
• **telephone: 1-800-730-2214**
• **fax: 1-800-730-2215**
• **web: http://www.thomsonrights.com**

**Library of Congress Cataloging-in-Publication Data**

Seguin, James A.
    Business communication : the real world, and your career / James
A. Seguin.
        p.    cm.
    ISBN 0-324-01426-0 (alk. paper)
    1. Vocational guidance--United States.  2. College students-
-Vocational guidance--United States.   I. Title.
HF5382.5.U5S43  2000
650.14--dc21
                                                           99-16248

This book is printed on acid-free paper.

# CONTENTS

## ACKNOWLEDGMENTS

I have had wonderful help in preparing this manuscript for publication. Dave Bennett, Ruth Hoffman and Dave Majka of the Robert Morris College Library provided a plethora of research suggestions. In addition, Dave Majka contributed substantially to the section, "Becoming a Wizard at Finding Answers to Questions." My colleagues, Tom Marshall and Bob Skovira, were kind enough to read the early proposals and open my eyes to unthought of possibilities. Coleman Myron assisted with copy editing. Nicole Ciamelle, who is an able and cheerful member of our Communications Department, was helpful in so many aspects, but especially in solving computer-related problems as was Connie Serapiglia. My heartfelt thanks to them all.

**Communication is the most important skill in life.**

**Stephen Covey**

**Preface.** Do yourself a favor. Get comfortable and read this book in "one fell swoop." Read fast and let the ideas soak through you. Your goal is to find a few important themes and an action plan--because this book is about you--about who you are at the core, what career goals you have and what you are willing to do to achieve these goals. You will not find a single paragraph about how to write a persuasive letter or give a dynamic sales presentation. They are extremely important skills, ones you need to learn, but not the subject of this book. The suggestions included here will serve you well no matter what field of business you are planning to enter or what job you are shooting for. The reality is that you can figure out some of the basics of communication early in your career and use this learning to your benefit--like making more money, buying a better house or nicer car, eating in fancy restaurants, making your high-school friends jealous, feeling better about yourself and getting promoted more often--or you can wait and discover--after years and years of trial and error--that unfocused communications skills can hurt you and your advancement. The choice is yours.

**Introduction.** In the cold dawn light along the banks of the Youghiogheny River, rows of huge black rubber rafts were lined up neatly. Small groups of people were warming themselves and listening intently to the instructor explaining the rigors of white-water rafting. "The river is high, and the rapids will be strong and rough. Follow my directions explicitly." That April morning I stood in one of those groups, wondering why I had decided to go on this trip. With the quick explanations done, our leader had us get in the raft and practice paddling and following his commands. His last command was something like, "The most important thing you can do is to keep your raft aligned with the river." In other words, don't go sideways or you'll flip over.

Soon after, we launched our raft into a fairly calm eddy. At first, the experience was easy, but as we hit the rapids, slid over rocks and dropped sharply over waterfalls, we were acting only on instinct We kept his words about staying aligned with the river in mind And by doing that, we averted disaster after disaster and got better as we went along. Three hours later, wet and tired, we enjoyed hot coffee and ham and cheese sandwiches while we recounted how great the trip was and how we were ready to do it again. The experience reminded me of trying to teach students about good communications skills. Instructors explain and you listen; then you practice skills through internships or a job. It's all helpful, but one key fact stands out--*the intensity of the real world is far beyond anything experienced in college.*

Perhaps there are ways educators can prepare students better for the real-world challenges of business. This is why I am interested in discussing a set a very different skills, skills that come first and are essential for effective communication. The 1990s have brought huge changes in the ways business is conducted. Methodical planning, traditional financial assumptions and rigid chains of commands have given way to creative problem solving, quick analysis of market trends and flexibility in all matters. As a friend of mine at a radio station says, "Problems don't disrupt a daily routine. They are the routine." If you ask someone to tell you about a typical day, you'll almost always get an answer like, "There is no typical day." Some people thrive in this environment--even enjoy it. Deals get done, deadlines are met, problems are solved, products and services are sold and money is made. These highly successful individuals know what to communicate, when to do it and how best to get their points across--even when they are tired, even in a crisis, and even when big money and careers are on the line. They maneuver, perhaps not always with ease, but with clear direction and leadership through the troubled waters.

These are not super human people--they make mistakes and get angry. But overall, they have developed a solid foundation that allows them to be an exceptional communicator on a day-to-day basis. What do these people know and what have they done to give themselves an ability to stay on course? That's what this book is about. In my more than 20 years of experience working for corporations and other organizations, I see three essential traits that excellent business communicators possess.

1. They have established a set of ground rules that guides them through the challenging daily activities of business.

2. They have developed an exceptional understanding of the business they're in, an understanding that provides a context for all their decisions and communications.

3. And they know how to choose the most effective communications tools to drive an individual, a team and a business forward.

Most successful individuals were not born with these skills. And many were college students at one time just like you. Along the way, they learned how to keep their raft upright, aligned with the river, and make progress from one set of rapids to another. A big part of their success is communication--communicating goals and persuading people to strive for those goals. You have a chance to get a head start in developing these foundation skills right now. The first step is to change your way of thinking. Let me suggest you put your "college-mind" in a drawer and begin to develop a "business-mind."

**The college-mind versus the business-mind.** To get through college with your sanity intact, many students develop a quality "college-mind." A college-mind relies mostly on individual performance. Except for the occasional class group project, you don't have to rely too much on other people.  In fact, too much collaboration in college and you'll be accused of cheating.  Secondly, lecture classes and typical teacher-student relationships feed you information.  In college, if you soak up the information and test well, you're in good shape.  A third factor is that you, or someone you know, are paying for your college experience--you're not being paid to perform work.  Therefore, your motivation differs from a paid employee.

The business experience and therefore the "business-mind" can be quite different.  While individual effort is important, working closely with others in many different ways is common.  As you may know from working on teams in college, successful teamwork demands exceptional communication and people skills.  Sometimes it may seem easier to do the work yourself, but many business problems are so complex they demand the ideas and action of many.

There are normally no lectures in business telling you exactly what to do.  Expectations are often unclear.  The responsibility falls on your shoulders  to define goals, determine what information you need and establish procedures.  Taking the initiative--not waiting to be fed assignments--is a key factor of the business mind.  Responding successfully to these challenges on a daily basis is what work entails.

The power and meaning of the pay check is under-rated.  People take their work seriously--much more seriously than students take their college responsibilities.  And the fact that careers, promotions and success are all intertwined makes the workplace a highly charged social-political environment.  You could say it's the human side of business and life.  Put a big-money project on a tight deadline with teams working feverishly, for example, to launch a new product, and you will be in the white-water part of the river working on guts and instinct.  It is here that your communication and people skills come under the test.  It is here where you need to know what guides you to make good decisions--to take risks where they are worth taking, to persuade others to follow your lead, or to hold back where you need to hold back.  How do you know what to do?  And how do you communicate it? Chapter 1  provides you with 12 questions to help you establish your own ground rules, so you'll have a better idea of how to do this.

In Chapter 2, we turn our sights from you and your communication skills to information. What do you need to know and how can you know the right stuff? Since there is so much to know today, how can you possibly ever know enough? More than before research skills are required and these are reviewed. But more importantly, this section discusses the significance of putting your business knowledge in context. You need to know a great deal about your industry, your company and your competitors; you also need to know about popular culture, current events and history. What to read, to do and who to know are discussed in this chapter.

Chapter 3 concentrates on what you can do as a college student outside the classroom to improve your communications skills, such as joining a professional association or planning a successful internship. Of course, you know that the world of communications technology is changing rapidly. Chapter 4 focuses on these technological advancements that allow you to communicate more visually or use multimedia communications. How can you improve your communications by creating more compelling documents, by using digital pictures, presentation tools or participating in networked meetings?

In case you want to know more about specific communications techniques and organizations, Chapter 5, the final chapter, lists resources: professional organizations, trade magazines, web sites, communication's company directories, and basic references for learning more about advertising, public relations, business communications, marketing, meeting planning, television/video and radio, and training and development.

# CHAPTER 1

# Establish Your Own Ground Rules

**The Twelve Questions**

**1. Who Are You and Where Are You Going?**

To be successful, you must come to an understanding of who you are, what you want out of work and life, and where you want to end up. Did you ever take a trip and not know where you were going? It's a ridiculous way to proceed unless you're roaming back roads for the fun of it. To reach a destination you have to have one in mind. But many people don't have any destination in mind whether it's for their life or their career. While you can't determine your life's actual end goal, you certainly can map a desirable path. This does not mean that you have to know now what you're specific career will be. It takes longer for some to figure out. That's okay. But now is the time to start settling on more specific goals; otherwise you will be traveling aimlessly, lessening your chances of a fulfilling career.

You can put some immediate direction in your life by writing your own mission statement. A mission statement is a paragraph explaining your goals. I know from having students write personal mission statements that I may have to convince you that this is worth doing. The way I see it--you really have no choice. There's an old ad campaign about putting good motor oil in your car. The saying from the mechanic in the ad was, "Pay me now, or pay me later." Pay a few dollars for the oil now or big repair bills later. And this is what I say to you about setting down a mission statement in writing--do it now and save yourself great deal of aggravation or do it later and wish you hadn't waited.

Another incentive to write your own mission statement is this: In a way, it's already written! You're not going to write just any mission statement--you're going to discover the one that's inside of you. It's been guiding you and growing with you. Now it's time to find it, bring it to the surface so that you can understand, evaluate and improve it. As you may know, mission statements are common in business--for companies, departments, project teams and individuals. When a company has a mission statement, then other departmental and individual statements can be created which also align with the company's overall mission. Specific goals, strategies and action plans follow so that these missions can be accomplished. It makes a certain amount of sense, doesn't it? Everyone working toward the same overall goal--how rare that is. You need to go through the same process--define an overall goal, then devise strategies to reach that goal.

Contrary to popular opinion, corporate mission statements do not need to focus on profit or maximizing shareholder wealth. Many have no financial goals in these statements. In their brilliant book, *Built to Last: Successful Habits of Visionary Companies*, James C. Collins and Jerry I. Porras studied the success of 18 exceptionally successful companies, including 3M, American Express, Boeing, Ford, General Electric, Proctor & Gamble, Sony, Wal-Mart and Walt Disney. These companies established a core ideology which can be found in their mission or values statements or credos. It's interesting that not a single one of these companies made profit the central theme in any of these documents. Collins and Porras believe this is so because "the drive for progress arises from a deep human urge--to explore, to create, to discover, to achieve, to change, to improve." [1] Aren't these feelings the ones that motivate you, too?

In its Values Statement the pharmaceutical giant, Merck, emphasizes that it is in the "business of preserving and improving human life." The company also states that "they expect profits, but only from work that satisfies customer needs and benefits humanity." The statement ends with this thought:

> We recognize that the ability to excel--to most
> competitively meet society's and customers' needs--
> depends on the integrity, knowledge, imagination, skill,
> diversity and teamwork of employees, and we value
> these qualities most highly. To this end, we strive to create
> an environment of mutual respect, encouragement
> and teamwork--a working environment that rewards

commitment and performance and is responsive to the needs of employees and their families.[2]

Merck has found a way to combine lofty goals with a strong work ethic and imagination. General Electric also has a Values Statement. It is simple, direct, energetic and quite specific:

Our Values

GE Leaders, Always with Unyielding Integrity:

*Have a passion for excellence and hate bureaucracy;

*Are open to ideas from anywhere and committed to Work-Out;

*Live quality and drive cost and speed for competitive advantage;

*Have the self confidence to involve everyone and behave in a boundaryless fashion;

*Create a clear, simple, reality-based vision and communicate it to all constituencies;

*Have enormous energy and the ability to energize others;

*Stretch, set aggressive goals and reward progress, yet understand accountability and commitment;

*See change as opportunity, no threat;

*Have global brains and build diverse and global teams.[3]

If those two statements don't give you ideas about your own mission in life, perhaps Sony's will. Sony espouses a different approach in its "Sony Spirit" statement. In his book about the early years of Sony, Akio Morita, Sony's co-founder, explains the origin and meaning of the statement.

In the very beginning, we had no company song..., but we did have a statement called the "Sony Spirit," a statement in which we believed. We first said Sony is a pioneer and that it never intends to follow others. "Through progress, Sony wants to serve the whole world," we said and went

on to say that in doing so the company would be "always
a seeker of the unknown." We also said this: "The road of
the pioneer is full of difficulties, but in spite of the many
hardships, people of Sony always unite harmoniously
and closely because of their joy of participating in creative
work and their pride in contributing their own unique talents
to this aim.[4]

If it's common for a business to put its positive foot forward in a
mission statement, it's fine for you, too. You need a simple, big,
positive, inspiring goal in life--you already know what it is, so put it
down on paper and get on with it. Perhaps it will make you feel
vulnerable to see it in black and white. I debated as to whether to put
my own mission statement in this book for all to see, but a good mission
statement is a proper and necessary starting point. As you write yours,
be sure to put a few specifics in. These specifics will help keep your
statement from getting too flowery and vague. Remember, there is no
right way or right goals, they need to be right for you. Below I've
included my mission statement.

### Mission Statement--Jim Seguin

I will be the best teacher I can be. I will help students to learn what they need to learn
so they will be prepared for the world of work and day-to-day life. In the classroom,
I will strive to create an atmosphere that encourages students to participate, confront
important issues and think creatively to solve problems. I am committed to fair and
high standards in learning and grading and will require students to meet these
standards.

I am committed to learning new technologies and better teaching methods. I will take
seminars and seek other opportunities that will help me do this. I will provide
evaluations to students and implement improvements when I can. I am interested in
maintaining a positive attitude and a creative spirit which will enrich the lives of
students, faculty and staff at Robert Morris College.

I will advance scholarship by writing useful papers and by attending professional
conferences. At these conferences I will meet and learn from as many attendees as
is possible. I will serve on two college committees a year. Each year, I will meet with
at least five potential incoming freshman, providing tours and information about the
communication program. I will provide letters of recommendations for students as
often as I can and assist students with finding jobs.

I will try to balance family and career as best I can.  And I will try to keep my job as enjoyable as possible!

What has this mission statement done for me, my students and the college where I teach?  It's made me realize how I must constantly strive to improve in teaching.  I've put it down on paper that I'm going to the best teacher that I can be--so I had better take student critiques seriously and work to keep my classroom style fresh.  Because of the statement I have sought more opportunities to help students with jobs and I believe I respond faster and provide more ideas to them when asked.  If current students tell prospective students about the educational opportunities at Robert Morris College, then it may increase enrollment.  Note also that I've included a few specific goals.   This adds the important reality factor.

But let's not take this too far.  Balance in all you do.  A mission statement is not in front of you everyday.  You may keep it in a drawer or inside a computer.  On a day-to-day basis you are not thinking about it.  So what good is it?  If you believe in what you wrote, it becomes part of you.  Sometimes you are aware of it and it guides you and sometimes not.  But it does affect you, those around you and your company.  By writing it down, you have taken a very important step-- you have become conscious of it and made it better.  How do you go about writing your own statement?  Find a time when you're relaxed and by yourself, and try writing down a few key ideas.  Build those ideas into coherent statements.  Then come back to it a few days, even a few weeks later.  Change it, make it better.  You may find this turns out to be a very satisfying experience, revealing things about yourself you weren't quite sure of.  The very process of working on your own mission statement is worthwhile because it makes you think about what is important and what is not.

**Write Your Own Retirement Speech.**  Am I crazy?  Okay, it's a bit on the wild side, but I guarantee it will get you thinking about directions in your life.  I had to do this when I was in graduate school and it was the most memorable assignment of my graduate studies.  I have students in my management class do this and the retirement speeches are given during the last class.  It's the highlight of the semester.

Although you may have to write your retirement speech outside the classroom environment, it can still be a valuable exercise for you. If you decide to do this, make sure you dream a little. You can end up as a billionaire and a philanthropist. You can start a company which will rival Microsoft. The speech is to be no more than three pages and it helps to write it in the third person as if it's being given by a colleague or friend. What would you like someone to say about you at the end of your career? What would you like to accomplish? When you start to do this, you may find how important these questions are to you. And it just may change the way you think about your career and how you will communicate with people on a daily basis. Try it. I dare you.

## 2.   Are You Cautious or a Risk-Taker?

> Far better it is to dare mighty things, to win glorious triumphs, even though checkered by failure, than to take rank with those poor spirits who neither enjoy much nor suffer much, because they live in the gray twilight that knows not victory, nor defeat.[5]
>
> Theodore Roosevelt, 1899

Former President Roosevelt's wonderful quote has and will continue to inspire many. I've always been a bit of a risk-taker, and in most cases these risks have paid off. But each risk had to be evaluated in terms of my goals before I ventured forth. Consider your own tendencies and past behavior--have you generally been cautious or have you tried to challenge yourself? You probably have established a pattern and see yourself as one or the other. Put that evaluation on hold for a moment. Let's return to thinking about your mission statement--isn't it really a foundation statement establishing your core ideology? Once you have established this solid foundation, you can take risks because you know what you are risking. If you fall you still have your foundation to land on. That's the key. You should never do anything which will violate your core beliefs about how to live and work. What you are risking, whether you succeed or fail, will not change your overall goals.

You may change your major in college and the type of job you're willing to accept after college. Many college graduates end up in industries and jobs that they never thought about while in college. And people commonly change careers.  A friend of mine is very happy in his fourth career.  He began as an industrial designer; then worked in sales and project management for a communications firm; after that, he became a top speech writer for a CEO of a Fortune 500 company; and now runs a consultancy business.  He may have one other change in him, he told me, to become a playwright.  Each change involved risk, but his overall goal was to design and express himself creatively through communications.  Even industrial design for him was a kind of creative communication.  He was comfortable with each change because his core ideology and end goal remained unchanged.

Even so, you could probably say that he had a high tolerance for risk. The terms "cautious" and "risk-taker" are relative terms and you can't say that one is better than the other.  Some people are more comfortable with risk than others; some invest in high-risk stock funds; others prefer more stability.  This will be true in business decisions, too, but I'm afraid you can't avoid risk.  If you're naturally cautious, you're going to have to find ways to take reasonable risks.  Sam Walton, the founder of Wal-Mart, has an interesting view on this, "You can't just keep doing what works one time, because everything around is always changing. To succeed, you have to stay out in front of the charge."[6]

In *Built to Last: Successful Habits of Visionary Companies*,  Collins and Porras suggest that companies come up with BHAGS--Big Hairy Audacious Goals.[7] BHAGS are goals that you can get excited about.  A goal with no pizazz, one you have no feeling for is not going to motivate you.  But one that lights you up, now that's something you can work toward.  Goals are going to differ greatly, but somewhere along the line find a big goal to go after.  Henry Ford wanted the automobile to be affordable for everyone; David Sarnoff, one of the founders of RCA, envisioned a radio in every home; Martin Luther King sought equality for all Americans; and Stephen Jobs, the co-founder of Apple Computer, wanted to improve education through easy-to-use personal computers.

I remember vividly President John Kennedy's statement about his intention to land a man on the moon: "...that this Nation should commit itself to achieving the goal, before this decade is out, of landing a man on the moon and returning him safely to earth."[8] I thought President

Kennedy was dreaming to think such an endeavor could be done--yet it was done--and it was a goal that excited the entire world. In your own career, think about a few BHAGS for yourself, integrate them into your mission statement. Even if you never achieve them, perhaps these "reach-goals" will stretch you further than you ever thought possible.

## 3.  Will You Initiate or Follow?

The day before you walk into your first big job, decide initiative is your middle name. I'm convinced from hiring college graduates that if they come to work with only one skill, I would want it to be initiative. The college-mind often puts this skill toward the bottom of the list; the business-mind puts it at the top. According to Robert E. Kelley in *How to Be a Star at Work,* initiative heads the list when co-workers and managers evaluate a new hire.[9] Since managers are basically problem-solvers, they're looking for people who can help do this. If you just sit there as if you're still in a college classroom waiting for assignments, you're part of the problem--not the solution. Colleagues look for new hires to pull their own weight. Otherwise, they know the day is coming when they'll have to do your part and they already have enough to do. So while showing initiative is critical, remember, it is also an exercise in good judgment. Pitch in where it makes sense to do so.

Let's take a common and not very important problem. Suppose someone is having a hard time finding a paper jam in the photocopier and you're not that busy. It seems the other person is on a deadline. You offer to help. This may seem like a simple act of kindness, but it is much more. Your offer recognizes that your colleague's time is important, that there is a problem to be solved, that the goals of a project, department or the business are being interrupted...so you lend a hand. It won't be forgotten. Initiative has other benefits, too, since it may encourage you to widen your social networks and friendships. Having relationships with colleagues is satisfying. And when the time comes when you need help, you'll probably get it. If you consider initiative to be doing the work no one else wants to do and you accept it begrudgingly, you're not thinking creatively enough. Initiative means that you embrace the tasks and be charged with positive energy. The specific type of work often doesn't matter; what matters is that you are placing the organization's goals above your own.

Of course, certain types of initiative result in spectacular results. For example, some people can see a problem that a lot of people in the organization face, but no one is trying to solve: For instance, suddenly Company ABC's products are suffering higher than average damage during shipping. The shipping manager has tried switching delivery companies, but that hasn't helped. Since the problem is sporadic, it goes unsolved. Let's say you have worked in the shipping area and you've decided that in your off-time to make a systematic analysis of the problem. You not only investigate the delivery companies, but you look at your company's packaging. What you find is that the product went through a redesign, and the packaging did not, causing undue pressure on the product's surface. A simple redesign of the package solves the problem, eliminating the ire of customers and reducing replacement costs. A string of such initiatives and you will be communicating the right stuff for a promotion. There are plenty of problems like this, problems which fall between the cracks. But, remember, don't let your initiative in solving these problems interfere with fulfilling the responsibilities of your own job.

You can see that taking initiative with a photocopy paper jam or solving a shipping problem costing the company money are quite different initiatives. One is helpful, the other is more closely aligned with the financial success of the company and so will gain greater visibility with higher-ups. As you become more experienced and able within a company, solving problems aligned to the company's mission will be more worth your while to work on. But remember, where to apply your initiative is a judgment call. You must have the expertise to solve the problem. Ventures that are likely to fail or cost the company large amounts of money are not worth the risk. Think about including the idea of initiative in your mission statement.

## 4.   Do You Believe You Can Solve Every Problem You Face?

If work is anything, it's problem-solving so your attitude toward problem-solving and your role in it needs serious self-evaluation. What's your approach...do you like to take the lead and find solutions or are you someone who is content to let others do that kind of work? If you have not been active in problem-solving when it confronts you, take heed.  Think about the exceptional problem-solvers you know--any examples will do--from your family, church, friends, or people from your business experience.  Have you noticed that people who are at the heart of solving difficult problems have incredible drive and focus?  Perhaps they have a never-say-die attitude that you admire, an ability not to become discouraged by initial failures.  Why?  One reason is because they believe every problem or challenge can be solved.  They not only believe it, they communicate this belief persuasively to all involved.  And these successful individuals have established a track record so they know from past experience it can be done.

Consider examples from outside the business arena.  Two enlightening examples are from the U.S. Space program.  If you recall the Apollo 13 moon mission, or perhaps the movie, you may recall that the spacecraft's power and guidance systems were somehow crippled.[10]  With a dwindling oxygen supply and little ability to maneuver the spacecraft, astronauts Jim Lovell, Fred Haise and Jack Swigert faced the awful possibility of being stranded 205,000 miles in space.  NASA engineers on earth worked frantically to get the damaged, almost powerless, spacecraft home safely.  Although one proposed solution after another was found to fail when tested in their simulator, the team of engineers rose above conflict, exhaustion and discouragement with one burst of creative energy after another.  As you know, they did find an ingenious solution which enabled the astronauts to maneuver the spacecraft on far less power than thought possible and with sufficient oxygen.   The astronauts were then able to re-enter the earth's atmosphere and land safely.  It's one of the great chapters in our space program and an incredible example of what belief in solving a problem can do.  Get the movie, "Apollo 13," and watch it closely this time with an eye toward the phenomenal problem-solving techniques demonstrated.

The second example is the 1996 Pathfinder exploration of Mars.  The Pathfinder spacecraft and its tiny robot explorer, Sojourner, sent back incredible pictures from the surface of Mars, providing us with data and visuals we had never seen before.  However, just after launch, the Pathfinder spacecraft was found to have a mysterious communications problem dooming the project.  Realize that the failure of this mission would have been devastating to NASA's Mars exploration program.

The story of the mission and how teams of NASA engineers solved the problems is well told in the book, *Mars: Uncovering the Secrets of the Red Planet*.[11] It took dozens of engineers, brainstorming and experimenting for 20 endless hours before the communications problem was solved. Again, teams of people were working non-stop, believing that they could find a way to fix the problem. And they did.

Our daily problem-solving efforts may not be as heroic, but we can learn from their deep desire to triumph over any obstacle. We have to believe that every problem can be solved somehow. You may not always find the ideal solution, but you will usually find some acceptable way to proceed. This has been my experience, and the older I get the more I believe it. Becoming the problem-solver, the person with poise under pressure, the person who others can rely on, can turn a mediocre career into a spectacular one. If you have that ability within you, nurture and develop it to the fullest. First, turn up your belief that problems can be solved, then take a tip from Collins and Porras. They note that successful problem-solvers don't settle by identifying just one or two solutions–as in–"it's either this or that." They insist it's far more effective to find several if not dozens of possibilities merely by thinking in terms of "and."[12] Don't let this concept pass you by.

So many mangers think in terms of either/or. It's natural to do so, but in the complex world of business, you seldom have merely two alternatives. For example, a manager in a planning session could say, "We can either invest money in the new venture or we can create new markets, but we can't do both." When presented with a case like this, you need to learn to ask if this is really true? Is there a way we can invest money *and* create new markets *and*, perhaps, reduce costs *and* raise prices." Maybe. If you don't ask, it will never happen. The company may not be able to invest as much money or open as many markets as wanted. Perhaps part of the plan must be delayed, but you *can* take action. You can solve a problem and move ahead. That's the key--finding a way to jump hurdles and drive the business forward.

The problem with either/or thinkers is that they limit opportunity and destroy enthusiasm. "And" thinking occurs along a continuum. An advantage of using this method is that it's easy and can be done anywhere. A continuum can be sketched on a restaurant napkin or in the corner of your meeting notes--a fancy computer program is not required. In fact, alternatives can often be set down in minutes. In a continuum, you put the two opposites at either end of the continuum, then place alternatives between them as you think of them. Usually, you put the safer choices toward the middle and the more radical–the more expensive, higher risk--alternatives at the ends. "And" thinking is creative, positive and is more likely to find a path your business can successfully follow.

## 5.  Are You an Individualist or a Team Player?

Did you notice in the NASA examples that problem-solving was accomplished by teams, not by individuals? It's because complex problem-solving requires the knowledge and contributions of many different specialists. There's often so much to know and accomplish no one person can know or do it all. It's as simple as that. That may seem like a modern phenomenon, but that's not so. Teamwork has been common in American business and political life. The "team" in Philadelphia that wrote the American Constitution in 1787 was incredibly effective. Or the international team, headed by General Eisenhower, that planned the Normandy invasion in 1945 certainly provided us with immense benefits. As did the very different but productive teams that created companies like Hewlett-Packard, General Electric or USX. You can imagine some of the difficulties each of these teams managed to overcome and you certainly know of the triumphs achieved. No individual could have come up with the same results. That's the power of teamwork.

Many college students have had bad experiences with teamwork required in classes. You may have found that the few, the conscientious, and the hard-working got the job done leaving resentment towards those who didn't do their jobs. If you've had some of those experiences yourself, you might like the old adage, "If you want something done, do it yourself." But in professional world, it will be hard to avoid teamwork because the pace and complexities of business are forcing more work to be accomplished in teams. Despite the many accomplishments of teams, you may encounter negative attitudes towards teamwork even within many businesses. And there are reasons for this. Some managers assign teamwork to confirm preordained conclusions; others point out that you don't get paid more for working on teams even though your workload often increases; and many people just don't know how to act on teams--they assume the few loudmouths will get their way--and sometimes they're right about that.

Research confirms, however, that problem-solving groups often define more and better solutions than individuals. They bring together diversity in knowledge, skills and perspective. In a diverse world this can pay off. But special communications skills are required if you're going to be an effective participant in a group environment. It is very important that you learn as much as possible about the advantages and disadvantages of teams, the typical stages teams go through, and the interpersonal dynamics usually experienced. A person who understands team processes can have a significant influence on the performance of that team. Since the turn of the century, scholars have published thousands of books and research papers summarizing team procedures and techniques. Below I discuss a few of these.

Most groups are problem or task oriented. Whether they're large or small, work over a short period or long one, wrestle with creative or technical difficulties, they seem to go through a rational process of problem-solving which was discussed in the early 1900s by John Dewey in his famous work, *How We Think*. He listed six steps in the problem-solving sequence: (1) sense a problem; (2) define it; (3) suggest a solution; (4) evaluate the advantages and disadvantages of the solution; (5) accept or reject it; (6) and if accepted, implement the solution; if not, start over.[13]

Dewey is saying that people move logically through a process of defining a problem, searching for and settling on a conclusion. This seems to be true more so for some than others, but consider this carefully: if things are that straight-forward and logical, what makes team problem solving so difficult? Why don't we all see problems similarly or act similarly in a team environment?

About 50 years ago at Harvard, Robert F. Bales studied typical verbal behavior in problem-solving groups. His work is explained in his book, *Interaction Process Analysis: A Method for the Study of Small Groups*, published in 1950.[14] He placed people in decision-making groups, gave them tasks to accomplish, and then studied what these people said during their meetings.  While his findings seem like common-sense today, they were not at the time.  He found that he could categorize participants' statements as being task-oriented or relationship-oriented.  Examples of typical task-oriented statements are giving suggestions, opinions or information; or asking for information, opinions or suggestions.  Examples of statements focusing on relationships are seems friendly, disagrees or shows antagonism.  In other words, some team members concentrated on getting the job done; others helped people work together.  I'm sure you have seen both types in groups you have been in and both types have their functions.  The task-oriented people can drive the group toward a solution; the relationship-oriented people can grease the wheels so progress can be made.  The need for balance on a team is critical.  Balancing task-oriented and relationship-oriented working styles is one critical component of a productive team.  This balance allows for humor and humility to enter the picture so that group members can back off from intense conflicts and find a way to compromise.  As a team member or leader you need to value and encourage both the task-oriented and relationship-oriented individuals.

But it's not that simple.  Isabel Briggs Myers and other members of her family studied personality characteristics which bring us unique insights about people interacting.  On the first page of her book, *Gifts Differing*, she says, "all too often, others with whom we come in contact do not reason as we reason, or do not value the things we value, or are not interested in what interests us."[15]  Does this sound familiar to you?  Briggs Myers wanted to know why and she found out.  In studies that took over 30 years, she determined that three-quarters of the American population are extroverts and are interested in people and the outer-world–so teamwork may come more naturally to them.  Introverts are interested in ideas, connections and the inner world, and while it may be harder to get these people to contribute on a team–their insights can be ingenious.  She also found that some people prefer to solve problems intuitively, some logically; some people are quick to judgment while others are very observant of what goes on in the world and slow to judgment.  An important idea to recognize about these characteristics is that they are very strong within an individual.  Normally, you are not going to get a person to change.  Effective teams allow for differences among people and use these differences to balance a team and to get work done.

Think about your own personality characteristics. Are you more of an extrovert or introvert? Are you intuitive or logical in your thinking? Briggs Myers is not saying that you are entirely one or the other–you just prefer one method over the other. Whichever you are, recognize it and don't stop others from working differently from you. The different styles can mesh and improve relationships and teamwork. If you want to understand these differences better, read the first chapter of her book.

In *The Project Manager's Desk Reference: A Comprehensive Guide to Project Planning, Scheduling, Evaluation, Control & Systems,* author James P. Lewis has several short chapters on team problem-solving techniques that can be helpful to you.[16] For example, you can think of problems as close-ended or open-ended. Close-ended problems have a single right solution. Perhaps a machine has broken. It needs to be repaired. That's the solution. But most problems you face are far more complicated than that--they're open-ended problems which could have any number of different solutions. So defining the problem specifically is really the starting point of problem-solving. He believes that starts with asking questions about the problem to make sure it is well defined. For example, suppose I had a class in which all the students were receiving low grades on tests. I could give them a speech about how lazy they are or how bad their study-habits are. From the tone of my speech, you can see how I am defining the problem. But couldn't the problem lie elsewhere--in the textbook, in my teaching or in the test itself? Obviously, incorrectly defining a problem in the beginning can lead you down the wrong path. There are hundreds of tips like this in *The Project Manager's Desk Reference.* I highly recommend this book, particularly if you want to know about exercises that can be used on teams to enhance problem-solving.

Other writers, such as Robert E. Kelly in *How to be a Star at Work,* make similar points. Problems can arise anywhere with teams, but to Kelley the most common problem starts with a team's goals--they have to be defined simply and clearly, redefined as you go and be understood by each participant.[17] Goal-setting is a common and often difficult problem for students working on classroom team projects. Thus, one of the most effective contributions you can make on a team is to help set clear goals. This skill will be extremely valuable throughout your college and professional career. As you can see, we have come full circle. In 1910, John Dewey saw the importance of clearly defining a problem; in 1998, Robert Kelley agrees and expands on the necessity of proper problem definition.

When teams hit roadblocks, you should know about how to break those roadblocks, using special problem-solving and communications techniques. I have outlined some below.

1.      Nominal Group Techniques: In this approach alternatives are generated by individuals who each make their own list of possibilities; ideas are then written one at a time on a chart for all to see and discuss; finally, a written vote is taken.

2.      Devil's Advocate Techniques: During discussion, one individual is assigned the role of critic. This is to ensure that opposing views and weaknesses are properly considered.

3.      Delphi Technique: Participants in various locations respond to a questionnaire. A manager summarizes the answers and this summary is sent back to the participants so they can adjust their previous answers if they wish. This is a very useful technique when face-to-face meetings are not required or possible.

4.      Role Reversal: This technique is used when decision-making hits a seemingly unmovable roadblock. Participants switch sides and argue the opposite point of view from the one they believe. This takes courage and a willingness to experiment, but it can change perspective and initiate progress.

5.      Brainstorming: Groups generate as many ideas as possible in a free-form manner. All ideas are written down without criticism. Participants try to build on each others' ideas. This method is an effective way to produce many ideas quickly.

In addition to these techniques, James P. Lewis offers useful but probably less well-known ones in *The Project Manager's Desk*

*Reference*. He calls one process, "creative analysis." There are 15 techniques described. Here's one designed to help a group re-define its problem-statement or end-goal. For example, he suggests that each group member try to complete a series of statements about the problem they're dealing with, as follows:

   a. There is usually more than one way of looking at problems. You could also define this one as...
   b. ...but the main point of the problem is...
   c. What I would really like to do is...
   d. If I could break all laws of reality (physical, social, etc.), I would try to solve it by...
   e. The problem, put another way, could be likened to...
   f. Another, even stranger, way of looking at it might be...[18]

After completing these statements, members discuss them. This is just one of many techniques discussed in Lewis' book. As you can see, problem-solving and team work have been thoroughly analyzed.

Another important area of research to be aware of concerns the stages of team dynamics. Teams go through periods of euphoria and other periods of intense conflict. These periods are fairly predictable, and exceptional team players understand and use these stages to keep a team on track. *The Team Handbook* (second edition) by Peter R. Scholtes describes the four stages as follows:[19]

1.   Forming:  Team members test the waters to see what's acceptable. People are often excited about the possibilities and they start to define the tasks at hand and to divide up the work.

2.   Storming: This is a difficult stage in which people demonstrate dissatisfaction with the team's progress and with contributions of some individuals. Conflict about the direction of the team and the ways to reach team goals are normal.

3.   Norming: This is a time of reconciliation. Members begin to accept the ground rules such as their roles on the team and the schedule. People share information and work at building cohesion.

4.      Performing:  This involves accomplishing the work the team was set up to do.  By this time, members usually understand each other's strengths and weaknesses and use that knowledge to get specific tasks accomplished.   There is generally satisfaction with the teams's progress and pride in the team's accomplishments.

*The Team Handbook* not only explains these stages, but provides many other insights on teamwork.  For example, there are sections on methods for collecting data, on guidelines for running meetings, making effective decisions, and record keeping.  Remember, a savvy team member may have to contribute more in the area of team process if the team leader or participants don't have team skills.  That may mean making sure the goals are clear, the contributions balanced, and the progress monitored.  This demands practice, but an individual who can make teams work better in today's environment will be seen as a valuable leader.

At the beginning of this section I asked you to think about whether you were going to be an individualist or a team player.  It's an unfair question because you have to be both.  We have discussed at some length the skills necessary for becoming an effective team member.  Learn those skills.  But, by all means, be the individualist that you are.  The workplace still demands, and I believe always will, a great deal of individual effort.  Rewards are piled on those who excel.  So don't let teamwork skills interfere with your individuality.

Below are additional references which may interest you.   All are available in paperback and most are under twenty dollars:

*ASTD Trainer's Sourcebook: Teambuilding*.  Cresencio Torres, Deborah M. Fairbanks and Richard L. Roe (editor), New York, McGraw-Hill, 1996.

*Building Team Spirit: Activities for Inspiring and Energizing Teams*. Barry Herman, Ph.D., New York, McGraw-Hill, 1997.

*Inside Teams: How Twenty World-Class Organizations Are Winning Through Teamwork.*   Richard S. Wellins, William C. Byham, (contributor) and George R. Dixon (contributor). San Francisco, Jossey-Bass Publishers, 1996.

## 6.   Are You a Positive or Negative Communicator?

Positive communicators are rare, powerful and highly effective.  I am not referring to sweetness or a false positive attitude that usually turns people off.  I mean the ability to consistently see and communicate what's possible instead of what's not.

It's a bit hard to understand why so many people fall into a negative communication style which ranges from complaining about cafeteria food to predicting the downfall of every program a company initiates. I'm sure you know people like this from family members to colleagues At the extreme are people who are against everything and they seem to invest most of their energy telling others what's wrong with the world, young people, city government and so on.  These people resist change and since they see only the factors that bring failure or limit success, that's what happens.  Negative attitudes are as contagious as the flu in January, and soon whole groups of people have taken on a scoffing demeanor.  Many people don't seem to realize how negative they have become or how subtly destructive it is, so on it goes.  There are various degrees of this type of communication.  For those of you who want to get ahead, practice sensible, positive communications--search for and communicate to people what's possible even when that's difficult.  You will be recognized and appreciated for it.

Think about the great leaders in our history or ones you know in your community.  Leadership seems to consist of both a clear vision of what you want to accomplish and the communication of that vision. Accomplishing that vision can be done only by identifying positive strategies and carrying out those strategies.  It's a positive undertaking through and through.  Perhaps you can see a recurring theme that applies both to companies and individuals: *establish a positive, focused mission and then set out to accomplish that mission.*  Negative attitudes and the communication of those negative attitudes hold you and your company back.

One way to evaluate your own attitude is to review your written communications--are you using positive or negative language?  For example, are you writing memos or sending e-mail communications which say something like, "Let's see what we can work out," or are you saying, "If we can't work this out, there will be severe consequences." Be aware of your verbal communications, too.  In most cases a negative statement can be turned into a positive statement.  The advantages of using positive statements are twofold: they're often shorter and clearer; secondly, positive statements are more motivational.

In his best selling book, *The Seven Habits of Highly Effective People*, Stephen Covey takes the idea of being positive a bit further.  He combines positive attitude and positive action.  Take a moment to consider your own language and behavior from his active point of view. How do you approach life on a daily basis?  Are you a person who believes that the forces of business or nature control you?  Or are you someone who believes that you can make your own choices and thereby control the outcome of most events?  Covey calls people who believe they have very little influence over the world reactive.  They react to events and are likely to believe that "you can't fight City Hall." With that attitude, what can you accomplish?  On the other hand, people who believe their choices make a difference are proactive.  These people are not only positive in attitude, they are positive in their language and actions.  And from that positive approach, good things happen. Compare your language and your attitude with some of the reactive and proactive statements listed by Covey.

| Reactive Language | Proactive Language |
|---|---|
| There's nothing I can do. | Let's look at our alternatives. |
| That's just the way I am. | I can choose a different approach. |
| I can't. | I choose. |
| I must. | I prefer.[20] |

I hope that you can see the enormous difference between these statements, the attitudes they stem from and the likely consequences of actions that follow.  If your attitudes and language fall consistently on the reactive side, it would be worth your while to change both.  Reactive people are less likely to be successful communicators and business executives.  Reactive attitudes lessen initiative and active problem-solving, detract from effective teamwork, and they certainly don't contribute to motivating others.  How many leaders do you know who consistently say, "I can't," or "There's nothing I can do."  These statements lead down a dead end road.

Nevertheless, when I bring up the topic of positive mental attitude, many people misinterpret my message.  Being positive does not mean agreeing with everybody and or every proposal put forth.  A healthy dose of critical analysis or doubt is often called for.  In fact, the term, groupthink, has become common in business  because organizations that stifle disagreement often end up in trouble.  The term was coined by Irving Janis and is well explained in his book, *Groupthink: Psychological Studies of Policy Decisions and Fiascoes.*[21]  As you can tell from the name, the group pushes the thinking forward.  Individual dissenting voices or doubts go unheard.  In American history, there are two famous examples of groupthink which resulted in colossal disasters.  The first was the April, 1961 U.S. "Bay of Pigs" invasion of Cuba.  Although the invasion was thought to be carefully planned by President Kennedy and his cabinet, it turned into a fiasco.  In the aftermath, advisors such as Arthur Schlesinger, Robert Kennedy and others said that they had doubts, but got carried along by the inertia of the group.[22]

Groupthink is also blamed for the January 28, 1986 explosion of the space shuttle, Challenger, which killed seven astronauts, including teacher Christa McAuliffe.  It shocked a nation that only became more shocked when it was learned that the disaster could and should have been prevented.  It seemed NASA had launched the shuttle even though some NASA engineers thought conditions were unsafe.[23]  A groupthink atmosphere pushed the project forward smothering opposing ideas that should have been heard.  It takes guts to be the lone voice in the wilderness or to express the disadvantages of a plan your boss likes, but sometimes it's necessary and part of being an able employee.  The Bay of Pigs disaster and the Challenger explosion illustrate the dangers of timid behavior and communication.  It is your job to know the place of both positive and appropriately critical or dissenting communication.

If you are interested in reading more about positive mental attitude and how it can contribute to your success in life and business, I strongly recommend you read Stephen Covey's book, *The Seven Habits of Highly Successful People.*

## 7.  Can you Handle Conflict?

The workplace is full of conflict.  People take their jobs and careers seriously and will fight for what they believe in.  Conflict is a natural part of people working together.  Disagreement often results in the identification of more and better solutions.  Since conflict occurs in all work environments, it's best if you figure out how you can use and control your emotions in the workplace.  Let's discuss anger first.  If you are a manager and you use anger to motivate a team, it might spur people on or it might have just the opposite effect, making the situation worse.  I've seen few positive effects from angry outbursts and plenty of negative ones.  You need to be thinking ahead as to how you're going to control anger when it wells up in you.  For many of us, this is a life-long struggle.

In most businesses in the U.S., emotionally charged communications are uncommon.  Strong emotions can cause employees to lose focus on the main tasks to be accomplished.  Because of this, the tendency is not over-the-top communications, but just the opposite–holding your emotions inside resulting in under communication.  But somewhere in between is a better place to be--clear, open and frequent communications which can maintain an emotional balance.  For example, a common problem is that a team leader changes the project goals, but fails to inform the team members.  If this has ever happened to you, you know how unappreciated it makes you feel.  Put your feelings aside and take positive action.  Seek out the individual or team of people who set the priorities.  If you don't, you may be left with a grudge and over time this leads to anger and resentment.  Note how maintaining clear, well defined goals again rises to the top of good communications.  Superior communicators not only set specific goals, they constantly refine those goals and inform those who need to know.

Another common example: your boss often gives you work on Friday afternoons--visuals to be prepared for a speech or a business report with a Monday morning due date.  These last minute assignments cause you tension, often ruin your weekends and perhaps interfere with your personal relationships.  What's the best way to handle this?  If you have a mission statement which states that you want some balance in your life, then you are more likely to deal with a problem in a positive way. Communication which you initiate is the key.  Setting up a meeting with your boss with, "Could we get together to talk about the preparation of your speech materials?" is better than an emotional outburst at 5 p.m. on Friday evening like, "You don't expect me to work all weekend again, do you?"

Even if you have trouble standing up for yourself, here's a tip that may help.  Make a list of your possibilities.

* Do the work and say nothing.
* Ask for the material sooner in the week.
* Discuss having someone assigned to help you.
* Alternate weekend duty with someone else.
* Refuse to stay and suffer the consequences.

Now when you set up a meeting with your boss, you have solutions in mind.  You can see that neither extreme is going to work too well, so focus on the middle choices.  Remember, in any meeting where you are negotiating a problem similar to this, you are communicating first and foremost an attitude, one that you want to get the work done in the best possible manner and another that you are seeking to preserve your personal time.  We all know that planning how you will handle your emotions will not prevent all arguments or unpleasant duties, but it will reduce them.    If you learn early in your career to use your communications and to keep your emotions in check, you may not only avoid unpleasantness, but also alter your career path.  A couple of final thoughts about emotions in the workplace should be mentioned.  Angry outbursts in private are far preferable to those in a hallway or other public area.  Secondly, anger directed at a colleague is minor, but at a boss or customer can be far more serious.  And anger which results in physical contact can be devastating to a career.

## 8.   Should You Compete or Cooperate?

The idea that business is war has been around for centuries and is still common today.  If you take this model to the extreme, a company's goal is to eliminate its competitors--win and make sure its enemies suffer big losses.  Where do you stand on this issue?  Should General Electric, for example, try to annihilate its competition?   Should Toyota or Volkswagen try to put all other car manufacturers out of business?  If business is war, then, yes, GE, Toyota and Volkswagen should adopt aggressive strategies which will remove all competition.  But it's hardly possible and if it were possible, the idea of a single company supplying the world with cars or airplane engines would not be accepted for long.

While military style thinking, military-like organizational structures and tactics still abound, the late twentieth century has seen new business models--like game theory--being proposed as a new way to think about competition and the marketplace. Adam M. Brandenburger and Barry J. Nalebuff have coined the term "coopetition."[24]   Though I never suspected it to happen, I have often had to cooperate with my competitors.  In running a firm which supplied companies with video communications, I have had to give creative product to a competitor because a client decided to have the competitor re-use material my company had originally created.  The first time I was asked to do this, I resisted vociferously, but now I know that it's part of the game and positive business relations are fostered by cooperating.

For you, it's important to evaluate your own approach.  If you see business as war, and only war, your strategies, tactics and communications will reflect the "I win--you lose" attitude.  However, if you subscribe to business game theory, there can be many winners and losers.  I believe it's a more realistic model for business operations.

If you are in sales, and you operate from a war-room mentality, you will do anything to gain sales and take them from your competitors.  But the world of business is not that simple because alliances and cooperative agreements are often made with competitors.  When you read business newspapers and magazines, you commonly find articles about companies forming strategic alliances or striking agreements to share information with outside suppliers and customers.  Working in a global marketplace has increased both the number and creativity of competitors. And with technology being developed at such a rapid rate, alliances are needed just to keep up with change. Alliances which add to a company's knowledge and skill base are naturally attractive to companies. By forming the joint venture, MSNBC, Microsoft and NBC have proved this, as have AT&T and TCI in combining their telephone and cable television companies. Cooperation among competitors occurs everywhere, even on the college campus where colleges allow students to take courses at competing institutions in order to offer a fuller curriculum. Automobile companies buy parts from competitors. Computer hardware and software companies plan products so that there is compatibility that benefits many companies. Competition among these companies can still be intense in many areas. The key is to notice how competition and cooperation are used side-by-side to advance a company's mission.

Since the 1980s, many American companies have used programs like quality circles and self-managed teams. Such efforts require information-sharing, consensus-building and other cooperative team strategies. These certainly are not war-like activities and they are becoming more popular because they are paying off for companies. Obviously, they also provide some people the opportunity of greater involvement in decision-making. That may increase employees' satisfaction in their work. If these cooperative and participative activities are going to work over the long haul, they demand superior leadership and communications. That's what you should recognize and why you need to study and practice team-work skills. You may find that controlling and using your competitive and cooperative instincts is a life-long task, but one that must be mastered to be a superstar communicator and leader.

## 9.  Can You Embrace Diversity and Foster Equal Opportunity?

Can you embrace diversity and foster equal opportunity? Or are you planning to pretend that you believe in equality? Sexist and racist behavior and communications are destructive to people and to business. It's a simple premise that most Americans agree with on paper, but in reality it's a different story. Sexual harassment and racial discrimination cases fill our courts--and these are just the ones that make it into our legal system.  An even greater number of people file discriminatory complaints with the U.S. Equal Employment Opportunity Commission (EEOC).  In 1991, 64,000 people filed charges; in 1995 that number rose to 95,000, an increase of 49%.[25]  Simply put, if you do not treat people with respect and spread opportunity equally, you are endangering yourself and your company--and you are limiting the potential of your business.

In a diverse world, a diverse work force can bring perspective and strategies that a more homogeneous work force will not.  Although a limited number of studies support this claim, one recent survey conducted in April, 1998, by the American Management Association (AMA) in partnership with Business and Professional Women USA, found that "a mixture of genders, ethnic backgrounds, and ages in senior management consistently correlates to superior corporate performance."[26]  The respondents to this survey were participants in AMA's ongoing survey-by-fax.  While these respondents do not reflect businesses in the U.S. economy as a whole, the organization's membership employs one-fourth of the U.S. workforce.

Discrimination is such a complex and volatile subject that it is seldom discussed openly in the workplace.  Dealing with your own feelings and behavior is extremely important and sometimes uncomfortable, but it must be done.  The first step is to take a look at your own circle of colleagues and friends.  If you interact in an environment where everyone looks and acts just like you, then you risk the problems that stem from isolation.  Recognize this.  Remember, without personal knowledge of people different from you, stereotypes build up.  What can you do about it?  One strategy is to seek diversity in your relationships. Seek out others different from you for lunch, team members, brainstorming sessions, car pools, whatever.  It's a rare person who does this, but it can be a powerful addition to your life and career.  There is so much to learn from people different from you.  Diversity is one big reason for world commerce and travel.  Don't we visit foreign cultures primarily because they are different?

Another strategy would be to find a mentor who is a different race or gender from you.  As you know, mentors can help you navigate through many difficult business situations or provide you with a different perspective.  A mentor who comes from a different background can keep you from being blind sided by consequences you failed to consider.  And when you are working and communicating from a strong point of view of equality, you can communicate and act with confidence.

In the U.S. discrimination isn't just disruptive to individuals and business, it's illegal.  The equal opportunity or civil rights movement began in earnest in the 1960s and culminated with the passing of the Civil Rights Act of 1964.  Learn all you can about equal opportunity legislation.  Here's a review to get you started:

1.      Title VII of the Civil Rights Act of 1964 broadly prohibits employment discrimination.  It states:

> It shall be an unlawful employment practice
> for an employer...to fail or refuse to hire
> or to discharge any individual, or otherwise
> to discriminate against any individual with
> respect to his  compensation, terms, conditions,
> or  privileges of  employment, because of
> such individual's race, color, religion, sex,
> or national origin.[27]

2.      Equal Pay Act of 1963 (EPA) prohibits discrimination on the basis of sex in the payment of wages or benefits where men and women perform work of similar skill, effort and responsibility for the same employer under the same working conditions.  The Act has several specific clauses, including: (1) Employers may not reduce wages of either sex to equalize pay between men and women, and (2) A violation of the EPA may occur where a different wage is paid to a person who worked in the same job before or after an employee of the opposite sex.[28]

3.      Age Discrimination in Employment Act of 1967   (ADEA) protects individuals who are 40 years of age or older from employment discrimination based on age.   It's quite comprehensive covering any term, condition, or privilege of employment–including, but not limited to, hiring, firing,

promotion, layoff, compensation, benefits, job assignments and training. The Act applies to both employees and job applicants, but it covers only employers with 20 or more employees.[29]

4.      Title I of the Americans with Disabilities Act of 1990 (ADA), prohibits private employers, state and local governments, employment agencies, labor unions and education institutions from discriminating against qualified individuals with disabilities in job application procedures, hiring, firing, advancement, compensation, job training and other terms. An employer who has 15 or more employees is required to make an accommodation for the disability of a qualified applicant or employee if it would not impose an "undue hardship" on the operation of the business. Reasonable accommodations are such things as ramps and handicapped-friendly bathrooms. The Act defines qualified individual, disability, and reasonable accommodations. An HIV-positive individual is considered to be disabled as are people who have been successfully rehabilitated from alcohol and drug treatment programs and who are no longer using these substances.[30]

5.      Civil Rights Act of 1991 amended the Civil Rights Act of 1964 in part to reverse a Supreme Court decision that limited these rights and "provide adequate protection to victims of discrimination." The Act authorizes compensatory and punitive damages in cases of intentional discrimination, and provides for obtaining attorneys' fees and the possibility of jury trials. This is an extremely important amendment; otherwise sexual harassment law suits could be unaffordable for most Americans.[31]

6.      Pregnancy Discrimination Act. This is an amendment to Title VII of the Civil Rights Act of 1964. Discrimination on the basis of pregnancy, childbirth or related medical conditions constitutes unlawful sex discrimination under Title VII. Women affected by pregnancy or related conditions must be treated in the same manner as other applicants or employees with similar abilities or limitations. An employer cannot refuse to hire a woman because of her pregnancy related condition as

long as she is able to perform the major functions of her job. There are other important regulations about maternity leave, health insurance and fringe benefits.[32]

The job-related areas covered by this legislation are extremely broad, including: hiring and firing; compensation, transfer, promotion, layoff, or recall; job advertisements; recruitment; testing; use of company facilities; training and apprenticeship programs; fringe benefits; retirement plans and disability leave. Discriminatory practices such as retaliation against an individual for filing a charge of discrimination are covered.   Even employment decisions based on stereotypes or assumptions about abilities or ethnic group are covered, as are denying employment opportunities to a person because of marriage to, or association with, an individual of a particular race, religion, national origin, or an individual with a disability.   Title VII also prohibits discrimination because of participation in schools or places of worship associated with a particular racial, ethnic, or religious group.[33] Are you surprised by the breadth and detail of the coverage?

**Sexual Harassment**.  In 1980 the Equal Employment Opportunity Commission issued guidelines declaring sexual harassment a violation of Section 703 of Title VII, but it wasn't until 1986 that the Supreme Court affirmed the basic premise of the EEOC's guidelines.  However, sexual harassment was not big news until the Anita Hill-Clarence Thomas Senate Hearings in 1991.  In the suit, Anita Hill accused her former boss, Clarence Thomas, of sexually harassing her.  At the time, Thomas was a nominee for Supreme Court Justice.  The hearings were televised nationally to very large audiences.   Ever since, sexual harassment has been more openly debated.  Despite this, most people seem to know little about the law.  As you enter the world of work, you need to know. Here's a little background.

Sexual harassment is a form of sex discrimination that violates Title VII of the Civil Rights Act of 1964.[34]

* Specifically prohibited are *unwelcome* sexual advances, requests for sexual favors, and other verbal or physical conduct of a sexual nature. Note that only unwelcome sexual conduct that is a term or condition of employment constitutes a violation.

* These unwelcome behaviors constitute sexual harassment when submission to or rejection of this conduct affects an individual's employment, unreasonably interferes with an individual's work performance or creates an intimidating, hostile or offensive work environment.

* The EEOC's Guidelines define two types of sexual harassment and you commonly see these terms used in newspaper accounts of sexual harassment cases. The terms are *quid pro quo* and *hostile environment*.

*Quid pro quo* is a Latin term meaning "something for something."  A typical statement that falls under this term would be phrased, "Do this or else you're fired," or "Do this if you want the promotion."  In more formal language, sexual harassment occurs when (1) submission to such conduct is made explicitly or implicitly a term or condition of an individual's employment or (2) submission or rejection of such conduct by an individual is used as the basis for employment decisions affecting the individual.

A *hostile environment* is created if the unwelcomed sexual advances, requests, or other verbal or physical conduct unreasonably interferes with an individual's work performance or creates an intimidating, hostile, or offensive working environment.

Although *quid pro quo* and hostile environment harassment are different charges, they often get muddled together in actual cases.  This is just one example of what makes sexual harassment cases difficult to prosecute. As new cases occur, the courts will continue to interpret the law.  If you read widely, you will read about these cases and be able to stay current of contemporary thinking.

To help employees be aware of their rights, employers are required to post notices to all employees advising them of their rights under the laws.  Many employers develop a company EEOC policy which not only explains the policy, but also details who is in charge and how complaints will be handled.  Such an EEOC statement is often printed in the employee manual.  Many companies today are writing separate sexual harassment statements.  This statement should also be found in the company employee manual.   Of course, all areas of equal opportunity are extremely important.   Because violations are so frequent, every business person should raise his or her awareness of equal opportunity issues in the United States.  The Equal Employment Opportunity Commission can provide you with excellent materials.

A charge of discrimination may be filed at any U.S. Equal Employment Opportunity commission field office.  Field offices are located in 50 U.S. cities.  The website,  http://www.eeoc.gov, is quite comprehensive and allows you to print a wide variety of documents and educational materials.  Or you can contact the EEOC as follows:

Equal Employment Opportunity Commission (EEOC)
Publications Unit
2401 E Street NW
Washington, DC 20507
800-669-3362 (TTD 800-669-3302)
Phone 800-669-4000 for the office nearest you.

Even though the references below are intended for managers who are setting up company diversity programs, they are excellent resources for those who want to improve their own diversity skills.  For the most part, these are practical works--guides, how-to manuals, and collections of essays about real problems and how they were solved.  Even if you are just entering the job market, you can gain wonderful insights from any one of these books.  Most are available in paperback and can be ordered through a local or on-line bookstore.

*ASTD Trainer's Sourcebook: Diversity.* Tina Rasmussen and Richard L. Roe (editor), New York, McGraw-Hill Company, 1995.

*Capitalizing on Workplace Diversity: A Practical Guide to Organizing Success Through Diversity.* Richard Y. Chang, Irvine, CA, Chang Associates, 1996.

*Change Equation: Capitalizing on Diversity for Effective Organizational Change.* J. Renae Norton and Ronald E. Fox, Washington, D.C., American Psychological Association, 1997.

*Communicating in a Diverse Workplace: A Practical Guide to Successful Workplace Communication Techniques.* Lillian A. Kuga, Irvine, CA, Chang Associates, 1996.

*Developing Competency to Manage Diversity: Readings, Cases & Activities.* Ruby L. Beale (contributor) and Taylor Cox, Jr. San Francisco, Berrett-Koehler Publishers, 1997.

*The Diversity Director: Why Some Initiatives Fail & What to Do About It.* Robert Hayles (contributor) and Armida Mendez Russell, Chicago, Irwin Professional Publishing, 1996.

*The Diversity Factor: Capturing the Competitive Advantage of a Changing Workforce.* Elsie Y. Cross (editor) and Margaret Blackburn White (editor), Chicago, Irwin Professional Publishing, 1996.

## 10. Can You Walk in Someone Else's Shoes?

Empathy is a very complex but necessary skill for success in business. It begins with a willingness to listen and observe so that you understand something from another's point of view. Business activities--from product design to sales--require empathy; otherwise how could you understand what a customer wants? Self-centeredness, inability to concentrate on another's message or a lack of respect for diversity, all prevent full understanding of the problems and possible solutions. Maybe you know people who only pretend to listen to you. Replies to your comments often make it obvious that they haven't heard you. These are blatant occurrences of an inability to listen, but perhaps it's deeper than that.

Listening begins by having a desire to understand another's communications. You can apply this empathic kind of thinking to all phases of business. In a workplace where everyone agrees on the proper way to proceed, the need for empathy is perhaps reduced. But in the heat of battle that can occur in business, under the pressure of deadlines and changing conditions, the ability to see the other side of the coin is critical to making progress. Teams composed of myopic individualists will accomplish little; their communications will be closed and limited. However, people who see that there are different and perhaps equal ways to get to the same end may open a door for a team to proceed, a project to get completed or a new idea to reach the table. Developing empathic skills is not easy. It means that you must bump into and find ways to work with people who are different from you. Perhaps you'll discover that your way is not always best. Strong empathic skills can lead to bursts of creativity, consensus, sensible compromise and progress. Highly empathic individuals often make great leaders.

A second concept I call a "helping concept." It's not that well understood or taught in business schools, but it can set the stage for your own advancement. Making your boss look good is a common sense principle of business. Now extend that concept to make your team look good or your colleagues look good. In so many cases if you are the moving force behind progress, everyone will know it. If you can make decisions and complete tasks in a manner that benefits not just yourself, but a group, and you communicate that intention, people will almost stop in their tracks and eyeball you because it is so uncommon. If you're going to be helpful to other people, do it in a straightforward way and you will be rewarded in ways that you might not expect.

Once you realize the importance and effectiveness of empathic and helping skills, your communications will change. You may find that communications are more frequent, open and include more information. You may find that contributing and letting others take the lead sometimes works just fine for you. However, let's make sure you realize what empathic and helping skills are not:  they are not out-and-out conformity or complete sublimation of your ideas to others. Both empathic and helping skills require a balanced, positive, active approach to work--taking initiatives and voicing discontent when needed. The best part about adopting these strategies is that you will also advance yourself.

## 11. Do You Plan on Being Honest and Trustworthy?

Honesty and trustworthiness are the hallmarks of an exceptional communicator. This is common sentiment, but, let's face it, there are many breaches of ethics today. It seems as though I read about some every week...tax evasion, theft, bribes, false advertising, sexual harassment, fake resumes, unfair preferential treatment to individuals and so on. Both white collar and blue collar violations are common. It would be easy to be cynical about the state of ethics in business, but any reduction in standards is just plain bad for people and for business. The field of medicine has a universal code of ethics--the Hippocratic Oath. Unfortunately, business has no such code. Nevertheless, business is based on trust and respect for individuals; without these basic tenets of human activity, civilized commerce could not take place. The more people adhere to fair and truthful behavior, the better the environment is for business; the more people stray from ethical standards the more the environment becomes chaotic and the exchange of goods and services difficult. If you have no trust in a product or service, you will not buy it.

Defining and adhering to a personal ethical code is paramount for all business people. Yet most of us need help in thinking out difficult ethical questions. Where do you start? When I was in high school, I attended the meetings of Rotary International, an organization for business people. I've never forgotten its *Four-Way Test of What We Think, Say or Do*. The test was created by Herbert J. Taylor, a member of the Rotary Club of Millen, Georgia. When you're in an ethical dilemma ask yourself these four questions.

The Four-Way Test of What We Think, Say, or Do

* Is it the truth?
* Is it fair to all concerned?
* Will it build goodwill and better friendships?
* Will it be beneficial to all concerned?[35]

Another approach is suggested by Kenneth Blanchard and Norman Vincent Peale in their book, *The Power of Ethical Management*. They provide three different questions for you to consider:

* Is it legal?
* Is it balanced and fair?
* How will it make me feel about myself?[36]

The authors also explain their "Five Principles of Ethical Power"-- Purpose, pride, patience, persistence and perspective. Purpose is akin to your mission--an overall goal for which you are striving.  Pride has to do with satisfaction in your accomplishments and those of your family, friends and colleagues.  Patience is built on self-esteem.  If you are confident, then you have faith in yourself and are willing to be patient in your decisions and actions.  Persistence is just what you think it is--never give up!  The fifth principle is perspective.  It is "the capacity to see what is really important in any given situation." [37] You can see that these principles are inter-related.  For example, perspective is much easier to have if you have a clear purpose or mission, as is persistence.  Again, note that a mission statement is the essential starting point.

The above gives you examples of templates to think out ethical dilemmas.  Some companies provide their own statements which all of their employees are to know and follow.  Johnson & Johnson has a famous credo that is integrated well into its corporate culture through employee orientation and company training.  Take a moment to read it.

### Our Credo

We believe our first responsibility is to the doctors, nurses and patients, to
mothers and fathers and all others who use our products and services.
In meeting their needs everything  we do must be of high quality.
We must constantly strive to reduce our costs
In order to obtain reasonable prices.
Customers' orders must be serviced promptly and accurately.
Our suppliers and distributors must have an opportunity
to make a fair profit.

We are responsible to our employees,
the men and women who work with us throughout the world.
Everyone must be considered as an individual
We must respect their dignity and recognize their merit.
They must have a sense of security in their jobs.
Compensation must be fair and adequate,
and working conditions clean, orderly and safe.
We must be mindful of ways to help our employees fulfill
their family responsibilities.
Employees must feel free to make suggestions and complaints.
There must be equal opportunity for employment, development
and advancement for those qualified.
We must provide competent management,
and their actions must be just and ethical.

We are responsible to the communities in which we live and work
and to the world community as well.
We must be good citizens -- support good works and charities
and bear our fair share of taxes.
We must encourage civic improvements and better health and education.
We must maintain in good order
the property we are privileged to use,
protecting the environment and natural resources.

Our final responsibility is to our stockholders.
Business must make a sound profit.
We must experiment with new ideas.
Research must be carried on, innovative programs developed
and mistakes paid for.
New equipment must be purchased, new facilities provided
and new products launched.
Reserves must be created to provide for adverse times.
When we operate according to these principles,
the stockholders should realize a fair return.[38]

Johnson & Johnson's Code is a broad statement that emphasizes being a responsible business and community citizen. It's beautifully written and I imagine a powerful reminder that helps Johnson & Johnson employees keep things in proper perspective.

## 12. How will you balance work and family?

We all have our own working styles and have set a pace for our lives. I hate to admit it, but I'm somewhat of a workaholic and so I have to counter that tendency by asking myself why I work so many hours. I try to evaluate what I'm doing, eliminate what's not that worthwhile and try to keep my work life and family life in balance. It's a struggle for me and probably always will be because I like my work and I find it challenging. Other people see life differently and have set a different pace. That's fine. You have to set a pace that is appropriate for you. Sometimes you have no choice--there is much to do and deadlines to meet so you burn the midnight oil. For many people the demands of work are powerful, unending, often exciting, leaving home life at the short end of the stick. If you are this way, then excessive hours spent at work may be fine for a while, but those involved in a social and family network seem to struggle in finding the balance between work and home. Americans are known workaholics, working longer hours and taking less vacation than workers in all other countries, except for the Japanese.

Many people today are concerned about the frenetic pace of work, the long hours required by businesses, the intrusion of work into home life through cell phones, pagers, faxes and computers. If you read the Careers column in the *New York Times* or thumb through *Fortune* magazine, you find plenty of articles about people who have altered their career path to increase time for family. If you want balance in your life, you may have to do the same. The value of balance in your life is that both work and home life can enrich each other. Lessons learned and experiences enjoyed cross-over in unexpected ways. And because your life has some sensible pacing to it, your health and state of mind should be better. Perhaps the idea of balance could be part of your mission statement.

**The 12 Questions.** I hope you're coming up with a few answers to these questions. But enough about you. Let's see what information you need to know to become an excellent communicator.

# Chapter 2

# Know Your Business & the World Around It

### 1.  Be an Avid Reader.

First, what can reading do for you?  Oh, change your life and skyrocket your career into a new orbit.  I feel that strongly about it.  For many of you college life may reduce your desire to read.  You're supposed to read dozens, if not hundreds of textbooks over your college years and know the material well enough to pass the tests.  The wisdom of the college-mind is to read as little as possible to get by or to sample only those areas that interest you.  If you are an avid reader, I applaud you. The textbooks are crucial for learning the fundamentals of business, but for most of you, that leaves little time or desire to read newspapers, magazines, novels or whatever else interests you.

As you get closer and closer to the world of work, this is a huge problem.  The business-mind needs to be well read because reading provides context and perspective.  Exceptional communicators and decision-makers know much more than the specific responsibilities of their jobs.  They need to know popular culture, emerging trends and technologies, developments within their industry or specific changes occurring at their competitors.  Your knowledge may have to cross disciplines and cultures; it may have to be about sales and marketing although your specialty is information systems; it may have to include some new development within your own area of specialization that traditionally has held little interest for you.  How do you do all that? You read, and you read some more and you keep reading, because if you don't, you have no chance of gaining the depth and breadth of knowledge required.  And it's not information contained in textbooks; the information is going to come from newspapers, trade magazines, business magazines, company materials, special reports, and maybe novels or biographies of successful entrepreneurs and managers.

Let's first look at your specific choices in reading.  Because there is so much to read, you'll have to limit it to what you really need to read to

Let's first look at your specific choices in reading. Because there is so much to read, you'll have to limit it to what you really need to read to keep up. Your goal is to find a few good things to read and read them. Don't get overwhelmed by trying to read too much and thereby reading almost nothing. Below is a list and brief descriptions of newspapers, general business magazines, trade magazines and other important readings:

**\* What to Read:**

*The Wall Street Journal* is an incredible resource that tells you all about business, and throws in a few columns about human interest and movies and the arts.

In writing this section, I wanted to find a way to convince those of you who are not familiar with *The Journal* to read it. I planned to summarize what I learned in reading it for just three days. It's a good idea except I learned far too much to include in this book. Let me just give you the highlights. Since *The Journal* has been published for so many years, it has been sculpted into a superbly organized business reading extravaganza; the writing is excellent--in fact, the writers and editors know how to provide just the right amount of information and to find ways to relate it to you; the topics are wide-ranging, covering the key development of the day and an unlikely entrepreneurial story from a far-off corner of the world. No matter what business you're in or what your interests are, you will find pertinent and fascinating articles to read. You could benefit either by skimming *The Journal* or by a more thorough reading of the stories that you find relevant. *The Wall Street Journal* is divided into three or four sections, depending on the day of the week:

The front section has national and international breaking news combined with highlights of what's inside. One issue I was reviewing had a lead article about changing regulations for down-payments for home-buyers. This article briefly analyzes the history of down-payments, interest rates and home ownership rates so that you can see the degree of change. To the left of the lead article and depending on what day you're reading, you see a column titled *Outlook*, or *Work*

*Week,* or *Tax Report,* or *Business Bulletin* or *Washington Wire.* This column gives you seven to ten brief, interesting summaries.

The middle column often profiles a unique individual with a business twist. They range from stories on Mr. Pig, the porker symbol for Piggly Wiggly, a southeastern grocery chain, who has improved his image by shedding a few pounds, to another about an aviation archaeologist who searchers for remnants of downed jets near Lake Mead. Don't think these are isolated or bizarre reports that have little to do with you. The writers are able to find unique stories which combine a savvy knowledge of human nature, humor and business. While reading these articles, you may find an emotion stirring in you to achieve what these individuals have. Or you may see a connection or strategy that may be incorporated into a research paper or eventually benefit the business where you work.

Two columns to the left of the middle column always stand out and are entitled *What's News*; one provides summaries of ten to twelve articles about national business and finance stores; the other looks at world-wide business news. If you read these two columns only, you would get snippets of about 24 stories that are inside that day's issue. The final column at the left edge of the paper provides intriguing business stories, often behind the scenes information about takeover attempts such as Asher Edelman's attempt with the Taittinger Champagne family; another details a story about a sexual harassment case at PaineWebber Group in New York City.

Now I have described only the front page for one day of *The Wall Street Journal.* Are you beginning to see how incredible this newspaper is? Inside you will get other sections which may interest you. *MARKETPLACE* provides a corporate focus on developments in the tobacco industry, chemical business, entertainment, steel and so on. On Thursdays, an *INTERNATIONAL* section is also included which has wonderful articles, charts and maps. On Friday, you often see a *WEEKEND JOURNAL* with arts, entertainment, real estate and sports articles. The third section of the Journal is MONEY & INVESTING. It always includes charts on stocks, bonds, interest rates, the U.S. dollar and commodities. Plus, there are plenty of investment-related articles and the listings for the stock exchanges.

Sometimes there are special issues. The one on November 16 is entitled, *TECHNOLOGY: Thinking about Tomorrow*: There are 16 articles that consider changes coming in networks; smart cards and money; video games; movies, music, sports and telephones. There is something in this special section that affects your life and career! Try reading *The Journal* for a week. I hope you will be hooked or at least recognize how informative, entertaining and useful it is. The website for *The Wall Street Journal Interactive Edition* is http://wsj.com. This site charges a fee.

Another great read is *The New York Times*. For business majors who want to know more about the information and communications industries, I suggest you read the Monday issue of *The New York Times*. To begin with, the *Times* will keep you up to date on national and international current events just by reading the front page. On Mondays, however, the *Business Day* section focus is "The Information Industries." Subjects included are communication satellites, the rift between Microsoft and Intel over the development of a multimedia chip, an in-depth article on Microsoft's new MSN strategy, and another on *Time Magazine* publishing one-advertiser issues. The *Business Digest* highlights and describes eight to ten business articles that appear inside the business section. In the *Times,* you'll get broader coverage than *The Wall Street Journal*; The Arts, Sports, Leisure and Travel are a few of the sections that might interest you. The website is www.nytimes.com. As of this writing, the site requires you to register, but there is no charge. There is a fee for use of their archives. If *The New York Times* does not appeal to you, try *The Washington Post,* the *Chicago Tribune* or the *Los Angeles Times*. The Internet addresses for these newspapers are: www.washingtonpost.com, www.chicagotribune.com, and www.latimes.com.

Read *USA TODAY* for fun and to understand popular culture. With its four sections--*NEWSLINE, MONEYLINE, SPORTSLINE AND LIFELINE*--the *USA TODAY* keys on events and developments that affect a majority of Americans and appeal to our interest in entertainment, sports and money. The articles are short, the pictures are great and the use of graphics, charts and maps get high marks. It is a good place to start your reading and the paper is widely available in hotels and from street corner machines.  It is especially popular with travelers.  I like the editorial page because it provides the *USA TODAY* view on an issue, such as Defense Cuts, and an opposing view.  Often the paper interviews people around the country and includes their comments on an issue, along with the picture of each respondent.  Special issues highlight topics of wide interest.  The ads are terrific, especially the full-page ones or multi-page pullouts.  The website is www.usatoday.com.

If you have a strong financial or international interests, try *Barron's, The Financial Times or The International Herald Tribune.*

Of course, read your local newspaper.  How else are you going to know what's going on in your area?  But in addition, read a local business weekly because it focuses on business in your community and region You may have special issues that you need to be aware of that stem from state and local laws, news about your airport and transportation systems, environmental concerns and so forth.  Usually, these papers are published weekly and if you read one for six months or more, you will have a good handle on both the influential people and businesses in your area and the critical issues affecting the business climate.

Often, these weeklies focus on different industries and so will have at least one issue which will look at your specific industry.  They have other worthwhile features which are particularly helpful to recent business graduates, such as: (1) Top 25--a list of the top players in each industry which often include gross sales and numbers employed. (2) "Up and Comers" noting promotions and accomplishments of people in the region. (3) Many have a "Record" section which lists a calendar of events, conventions, seminars and the like; awards and honors; insider trading; bankruptcy filings; new business incorporations; new clients of Ad/PR accounts and much more.  They are also a good outlet for your letters to the editor or a guest article.  About 35 of these Business Journals are included in the website: www.amcity.com.  At this site you can travel to the various cities and get news, news briefs and opinion pieces for growing a business.  More than 1,000 items are posted weekly by local American Business Journals' reporters.

In addition, many journals publish other helpful books.  One I like is the *Book of Lists* which lists the top businesses by industry with other detailed financial and employment data about each.   Many have software versions of these lists which will allow you to print labels, follow-up reports and export data into your software programs.  Then there are *Business Directories* which provide more comprehensive information on the main companies in your area.

*BUSINESS WEEK* provides a wonderful and fascinating overview of business.   It's for the business person who has a curious mind, wide-ranging interests and a managerial perspective.  It is well-designed and easy to read.  I encourage you to take a look at its two-page table of contents and you will find a structure that most magazines have adopted, a combination of images and text outlining content, but in this case it is both clear and attractive.

Each week, *BUSINESS WEEK* has a cover story which might encompass two or three articles.  Typical cover stories are "The Future of the American Car," "Nokia: Can CEO Ollila Keep the Cellular Superstar Flying High?", and "How GE's Welch is Remaking his Company--Again."   They are well written, succinct and cover the people, key business challenges and developments which make reading the article a learning experience.   Following the feature story is a section on *News Analysis & Commentary* which focuses on important breaking news with long-term consequences.  Then sections vary from week-to-week which is one of the aspects I especially like about this magazine.  It finds hot subjects to key on so that if you read it over a year, you will develop a broad sense of business trends.   Whatever industry you're in, you can count on its coverage in *BUSINESS WEEK*.  Some of the section headings are: *International Business, Economic Analysis, Government, Marketing, Science & Technology, Finance, The Workplace, The Corporation, Social Issues, Management, Sports Business, People, Media* and *Information Processing and Personal Business*.  There are many more, but you can see the eclectic interest of the editors and readers of this magazine.  The magazine has weekly features like *Up Front*--briefs on interesting developments, plus *Book Reviews, Technology & You,* and *Business Indexes* which include production indexes and leading indicators.  I particularly enjoy the Annual Report which encompasses the entire magazine.  The one in

July, 1998 was on, "Doing Business in the Internet Age." It was a high-quality and comprehensive analysis of Internet business opportunities and challenges. In addition, the magazine's website is excellent and contains both free and fee-based services. The address is: www.businessweek.com.

*FORTUNE* provides a bit more in-depth articles than *BUSINESS WEEK*. While it covers a variety of business topics, *FORTUNE* places more emphasis on investment-related subjects. The sections are, *First*--topical business developments; *Features*--one  example was a look at the new industrial order emerging because of the Internet. Other articles were on the software company, SAP, and its enterprise software; Charles Schwab and how he has embraced the Web at his brokerage; and VF Corporation which is using several packaged software tools to alter its jeans and lingerie manufacturing. Other subject headings are *Techno File* and *Staying Smart*, both of which provide interesting information of interest to managers. Toward the back of the magazine are sections on Career Opportunities and a Classified Business Exchange. The website is www.fortune.com or www.pathfinder.com/fortune/. It offers a combination of free and fee-based services.

*FORBES* is a hefty, tour-de-force business magazine with an emphasis on management, money-making and investment strategies. One issue might have up to 50 two to three page articles plus standard features. A recent issue covers companies involved in artificial intelligence, satellite communications, airlines, E-mail, Pizza, Gambling Casinos and it includes a list of 500 Top Private Companies. While it is interesting and worth reading, it suffers from a cluttered look, making it harder to find your way through it than *BUSINESS WEEK* and *FORTUNE*. The website at www.forbes.com is full of information and includes access to their supplement magazine, *Forbes ASAP*. There is a plethora of other services at the Forbes website, including:

*   Forbes Private Companies Database: online company information by state, industry, revenue, and profits.

*   Forbes Wire Desk where you can check the pulse of the markets three times a day through the address: www.forbes.com/wires.

*   Forbes Small Business Center--data based on the magazine's Entrepreneurs department--you can ask editors questions in the online forum or e-mail them at www.forbes.com/growing.

*   Forbes Executive Women's Summit: It can be found at www.forbes.com/execwomen.

*   Forbes Digital Tool Newsletter. This is an e-mail newsletter which includes original reporting, market updates and highlights of upcoming articles. It can be found at www.forbes.com.

*   Forbes Perspective: Forbes Business Audio Series: You can listen to the latest news, insights and strategies at www.forbes.com/tool/tool-box/audio.

A few other worthwhile business oriented magazines to consider are: *The Economist, Entrepreneur, Fast Company* and *Inc. Magazine*.

In addition to *The Wall Street Journal* and the *New York Times*, consider listening to National Public Radio (NPR). The national news programs are: *Morning Edition*, which is broadcast from about 6 to 9 a.m. in many markets. The early evening program is *All Things Considered*, which begins at 4 or 5 p.m. National Public Radio has in-depth news and information which is nicely packaged, has a human touch, yet provides you with more in-depth coverage of hard news and major issues of the day. NPR also uses a wide range of content experts and commentators and, although no news is completely objective, they do a pretty good job of providing various perspectives. They also provide coverage of developments in music and entertainment--so you get more than news. The website is www.npr.com. If you visit the website, other programs you might be interested in learning about are: *Fresh Air,* an interview program with Terry Gross, and speeches broadcast by The Commonwealth Club of California and The Press Club in Washington, D.C.

Of course, national and cable television news can help keep you up-to-date. This includes: ABC, CBS, CNN, Fox News, and NBC. The *NewsHour with Jim Lehrer* (PBS) often provides more background and discussion on breaking stories. CNN's *Larry King Live,* and *Moneyline News Hour with Lou Dobbs* can be both informative and entertaining to watch. Sunday morning programs such as *CBS News Sunday Morning* are worthwhile. Don't forget about programs in the style of *Dateline* on NBC or *Frontline* on PBS. *Frontline* has provided excellent business oriented programs on subjects such as web advertising and Rupert Murdoch's News Corporation.

Internet news services are becoming more comprehensive and more enjoyable as editors learn what people want and how to design and deliver information through the internet. The following sites are recommended, although you will find many others.

http://www. precedes the following internet addresses:

| | |
|---|---|
| abc.com | economist.com |
| bloomberg.com | ft.com |
| broadcast.com | foxnews.com |
| pointcast.com | hispanstar.com |
| cnn.com plus | moneynet.com |
| CNN Interactive | msnbc.com |
| CNNfn | |

Many of these services will provide you with customized news based on your interests and then deliver this news electronically to your computer. These services are helpful for staying abreast of a specific industry, but beware of becoming too specialized and therefore isolated.

## 2.  Know about History

It may seem like I'm asking you to cover a lot of ground when I say, "Know history!" But hold on, don't throw the book across the room just yet. There are specific areas for you to concentrate on. First, how can history be that important? It is because history is the sum total of events and experiences which have preceded where you are right now. This is true for the college you attend, the company where you work or will work, the community you live in, and the people you live and work with. Each has a history and those past events affect you and the people around you today. For example, if you don't know the history of your community, then you may not understand why community members don't want taxes spent for a baseball stadium; if you are working on business developments that depend on the construction of a new stadium, then you need to know and understand how people feel about this issue.

To fully understand and appreciate current events, it's necessary to know the background of those events.  Also, it makes today's world more interesting.  Such topics as the European Community, growth of telecommunications, or the changing role of women in business are just a few of the subjects commonly found in the news.  They're neither boring nor irrelevant when seen in context.  Understanding that they are important in the world of business is one step; knowing enough about these and other issues is the next step; and integrating them into your business decisions is the third step.  Why?  Social events affect how people think and behave and therefore how they work and shop.  It's the foundation of business.  You can't learn everything about historical events in a few days.  Over time, however, if you're curious about the past, you can learn what's relevant for you.  You may discover patterns in history that relate to your situation and even better--you may be able to put that information to use.  By doing so, you become an improved decision-maker and communicator.  Let's consider world history first. I have selected a few books which provide perspective on key historical events and ideas.

## * World History

*A History of Knowledge, The Pivotal Events, People and Achievements of World History* by Charles Van Doren, Ballantine Books, New York, 1991.  This is a wonderful book, available in paperback, which takes you through ancient history, through the Greek and Roman World on to through the Renaissance, World Wars and into the Twenty-first Century. Its emphasis is on the major ideas that developed and changed the way we live and think.  It's easy and fascinating to read and inspirational.

*History of the United States* by Douglas Brinkley, American Heritage, Penguin Group, New York, 1998.  This is American history in one volume; it is nicely written, beautifully illustrated and looks nice on your coffee table.

*The Americans: The Democratic Experience*, Daniel J. Boorstin, New York, Vintage Books, 1974.  This is the first book of a Pulitzer Prize winning trilogy.  It paints a vivid portrait of post Civil-War America. *The Americans* may provide you not only better insight into our unique American democratic society, but also give you a stronger picture of your important role in it.

*The Oxford History of the Twentieth Century* edited by Michael Howard and William Roger Louis, Oxford University Press, New York, 1998. This is a series of essays by more than 20 scholars from around the world giving you interesting historical perspective on political, cultural, social, artistic, and technological developments of the twentieth century.

*Civilisation* by Kenneth Clark.  Kenneth Clark is a highly respected historian with a humanistic perspective.

If reading is not something you enjoy, you could try videotape series such as *The History of the Twentieth Century*.  Many videotape series, including those that have been previously shown on cable or broadcast television such as PBS, A&E, Discovery and The Learning Channel, can be found at your public or college library.

## *  History of Business

A great way to learn about how American business developed and how it operates is to read the biographies of successful business entrepreneurs and managers, and the stories of how new companies were built or turned around.  The commitment some business leaders have to their businesses is astounding; their creativity and drive continually surprises. You can learn a great deal by their triumphs and failures, and, equally as important, you learn about yourself.  Reading these works can strengthen your ability to problem-solve or undergo difficult times.  These important inner qualities can then be translated into better communications.  Below is a list of biographies of business leaders and corporate turn-around stories.  Just select a few to read or even skim from time to time.  Some are better than fiction.  Don't be alarmed by the publication dates which range from 1950-1999. Even those written decades ago are fascinating and well worth reading. I've listed these by title first, making this long list a bit easier to follow.

*A Business and its Beliefs*. Thomas J. Watson, Jr., New York, Columbia University Press, 1963.

*Aol.com: How Steve Case Beat Bill Gates, Nailed the Netheads and Made Millions in the War for the Web*. Kara Swisher, Times Books, New York, 1998.

*At Any Cost: Jack Welch, General Electric & the Pursuit of Profit*. Thomas F. O'Boyle, Random House, New York, 1998.

*Barbarians at the Gate: The Fall of RJR Nabisco*. Bryan Burrough and John Helyar (contributor), Harper Collins, New York, 1991.

*Building a Company: Roy O. Disney and the Creation of an Entertainment Empire*. Bob Thomas, Hyperion, 1998.

*A Company that Cares*. Lawrence G. Foster, New Brunswick, NJ, Johnson & Johnson, 1986.

*Citibank 1812-1970*. Cambridge, MA, Harvard University Press, 1985.

*Citicorp: The Story of a Bank in Crisis*. Richard B. Miller, New York, McGraw Hill, 1993.

*Donald Douglas--A Heart with Wings*. Wilbur H. Morrison, Ames, IA, Iowa State University Press, 1991.

*Eyes on Tomorrow: The Evolution of Proctor & Gamble*. New York, Doubleday, 1981.

*Father, Son & Company*. Thomas J. Watson, Jr., New York, Bantam Books, 1990.

*Ford, The Men and the Machine*. New York, Ballantine Books, 1986.

*Game Over: How Nintendo Conquered the World.* David Sheff, New York, Vintage Books, 1993.

*House of Cards: Inside the Troubled Empire of American Express.* New York, Putnam, 1992.

*IBM: Colossus in Transition.* Robert Sobel, New York, Truman Talley Books, 1981.

*Legend and Legacy: The Story of Boeing and Its People.* Robert J. Serling, New York, St. Martin's Press, 1992.

*Made in Japan: Akio Morita and Sony.* Akio Morita, New York, Dutton, 1986.

*Marriott: The J. Willard Marriott Story.* Salt Lake City, Deseret, 1987.

*Our Story So Far.* St. Paul, MN, 3M Company, 1977.

*Sam Walton: Made in America.* Sam Walton with John Huey, New York: Doubleday, 1992.

*Prince of the Magic Kingdom.* Michael Eisner and the Re-Making of Disney, New York, Wiley, 1991.

*Rude Awakening: The Rise, Fall, and Struggle for Recovery of General Motors.* Maryann Keller, New York: William Morrow, 1989.

*Soap Opera: The Inside Story of Proctor & Gamble.* Alecia Swasy, New York, Times Books, 1993.

*Speeding the Net: The Inside Story of Netscape and How it Challenged Microsoft.* Joshua Quittner, Michele Slatalla, and Josh Quittner, Atlantic Monthly Press, 1998.

*Storming the Magic Kingdom.* John Taylor, New York: Ballantine Books, 1987.

*Titan: The Life of John D. Rockefeller,* Ron Chernow, Random House, New York, 1998.

*The Chase.* John Donald Wilson, Boston, Harvard Business School Press, 1986.

*The Columbia Story.* Clive Hirshhorn, New York, Crown, 1989.

*The Founder's Touch.* Harry Mark Petrakis, New York, McGraw-Hill, 1965.

*The Immigrant in 1887.* John W. Nordstrom, Seattle, Dogwood Press, 1950.

*The New GE.* Robert Slater, Homewood, IL, Irwin, 1993.

*Turnaround: The Ford Motor Company.* Robert L. Shook, New York, Prentice-Hall, 1990.

*The Sony Vision.* Nick Lyons, New York, Crown, 1976.

*Values and Visions, a Merck Century.* Rahway, NJ: Merck, 1993.

*Walt Disney: Hollywood's Dark Prince.* Marc Eliot, New York, Birch Lane Press, 1993.

*William L. McKnight, Industrialist.* Minneapolis: T.S. Denison, 1962.

Remember, some of these books are also available as audio books. It's fun to listen to these as you drive to work or on longer trips.

## *   History of Your Industry and Your Company

A little creative research may be in order to learn about and appreciate the history of your industry. Certainly any of the books listed above from your area of specialization would be helpful. You may be surprised by what you can learn from encyclopedias and references such as the *Information Please Almanac, or The New York Times* or the *Wall Street Journal Almanacs.* In addition, your company and your competitors are probably listed in *Hoover's Handbook of Corporations* or the *International Directory of Company Histories.* These books can be found in the reference section of your library or on the Internet.

As far as your company, read everything you can get. It's important that you know the key milestones, setbacks and people of your company.

## *  History of Your Community

It's easy to learn about your region and community and it's especially important if you are new to an area. People are usually proud of where they live so look for the positive even if you're not enamored with the location. You will find resources at your local libraries, museums, in bookstores, at travel companies and on the Internet.

## *  Other Ways to Learn about History

While I have suggested that you read mostly nonfiction works, I don't mean to eliminate fiction. Novels, for example, do more than entertain; they can be the source of new ideas or stimulate you to reach higher with your life goals. Fictional accounts of events can sometimes provide you with insights that you won't get from the more serious non-fiction sources.

## 3.  Interact and Learn From Other People.

Developing relationships with a range of people--and finding time to talk with them about business matters and beyond--can be extremely helpful. You should start doing this in college, but for the purposes of this discussion, let's look forward to a time when you're in your first job. Below, three different aspects of people-interaction are discussed.

*  **Be visible.** Walk around and talk with people. It seems like common sense, but because of tight schedules both at work and home and the ease of computer communications, there seems to be less and less of it. Good things and sometimes unexpected things happen just because you are around and are seen. People value face-to-face contact today and someone who makes a special effort to do this will create simple surprises and light up a few faces. Productivity, quality and bottom line

orientation are all recognized as valuable; less recognized is personal, direct contact with people.  Make sure this kind of communication happens in your workday.  It's easy to do.  Instead of using internal mail, occasionally drop a report off in person.  Take the long way to the printer so that you pass a few different offices.  Chat with people along the way.  If you're not a people person, try to develop this part of your personality; it's really just connecting with people through communication, humor and common interests.  It's not that hard and as we move further into the information economy, people and face-to-face communication skills will be more important than ever.

* **Network.**  Networking is taking people interaction to the next level.  As you develop friendships notice those who are the movers and shakers within your company.  I don't mean those employees who just play the game well, but people who seem to have more than themselves in mind--people who:

* Have a grasp of the big picture;
* Are knowledgeable;
* Have wide, even cross-disciplinary interests;
* Are committed to quality in every thing they do; and
* Are creative thinkers and problem-solvers.

You may find that these individuals are the most fascinating people to be around, and your life is more enjoyable because of this.  But most likely it will go far beyond this.  As you build relationships you will be able to ask about problems you face.  At other times, you will be able to share information and ideas with them or assist in solving someone else's problem.  Relationships like these take time and are built on trust.  They work best with a free exchange of ideas so that they are mutually beneficial.  To be a part of this network, keep your mind fresh and curious, have the guts to meet and interact with a wide variety of people and be willing to commit the time to develop and nourish these relationships.

So far we have discussed interacting with a network of people inside your company, but equally important is to know and talk with people outside your company and your specialty.  This may be more difficult, but such relationships can come from professional organizations, people you meet at annual conferences and conventions, social events and so on.   A common term you are probably familiar with is "thinking outside-the-box."   Coined by Edward De Bono in his book, *Lateral Thinking: Creativity Step-by-Step*, it means thinking in ways outside your own world.[1]   This is a particularly important concept.   If you are surrounded by the same people, thinking similar thoughts, new and different opportunities may never arise.

In the 1980s, the American automobile and steel industries were thinking inside-the-box when they allowed Japanese companies to take huge chunks of market share from them; also in the 1980s, national television networks, ABC, CBS and NBC did not recognize the threat of newly launched CNN.   Even worse, the networks never had the vision to see the opportunity in world news delivery that CNN's Ted Turner saw.   What a colossal loss of business for the networks!

A more recent example was the 1998 Asian monetary crisis.   Peter Drucker argued in his article, "The Next Information Revolution,"  that computer information systems have turned managers inward.[2] The crisis was not foreseen, he believes, because managers' information was coming mostly from inside-the-box.   Data was freely available to predict this widespread financial downturn if only managers were looking appropriately outward and had taken note.

Some people resist networking because they feel uncomfortable about sharing information or asking questions of others.   It takes at least a little courage to admit that there is information you don't know.   No one wants to appear to be uninformed.   It's a natural feeling, but you are far better off to admit that you don't know everything and recognize where your deficiencies are.   We all have them and today it's true more than ever.   There is general agreement that there is simply more to know, more information to draw from and more change occurring at a faster clip.   If you read a fair amount, use the Internet and watch television, you probably have 50 to 100 times the information passing through your mind in a year than people at the turn of the century. Because of the information glut, specialists abound, but as you know, the more you specialize the less time you have to learn about things outside your specialty.   So, people-networking is an essential activity. Think of it this way: Networking is an enjoyable way to learn, a great way to share information, to help and be helped.

Being with people and seeing how others would solve problems may cut a wide path for you through the information overload problem. Throughout this book, I have emphasized how important it is to read. But from another perspective, what and how much do you really need to know? It's easy to get lost in the forest of information. Some individuals are almost paralyzed by the inundation of information. Networking can help prevent this, because a short talk with a networking friend or colleague can pull you out of the woods if you're lost. Another factor to consider is that technology and mergers have decreased the number of people available to perform the work required. I hear it all the time and from all types of businesses, "I can't get the entire job done nor have the time to read what I would like...attend conferences and still have a life." Modern business problems and typical knowledge-industry projects are complex, which often means you need to increase the brainpower to get the job done. Networking helps with this.

In his book, *How to be a Star at Work,* Robert Kelley calls the network we have been discussing, a "guru network." He devotes an entire chapter to the subject which I highly recommend you read.[3] Kelley emphasizes the importance of properly maintaining this network. It's hard to ask a favor of someone you haven't talked to in years. Exchange of information and other helpful services must be freely and gladly given in a mutual way. There has to be help for all at some time...and credit and thanks need to be freely given, too. Keeping this on the up-and-up is critical to keeping your network strong and healthy.

\* **Find a Mentor.** A mentor is someone you respect and who respects you, a person you feel comfortable to talk openly about a wide range of problems and concerns. Although people you network with may serve as a mentor, usually a mentor is someone you have a closer collegial relationship with.

Mentors can be especially helpful with the politics of the workplace. If you can become comfortable establishing relationships with people who are older or who are in prestigious or interesting positions, you may find one who is willing to act as a mentor.  While in college, this would include professors, older students who are working and attending classes, graduate students, people you meet on your summer jobs or during field visits, people from professional organizations, parents of friends, neighbors and so on.  Perhaps you are shy or feel these people are too busy to help you--these feelings probably come from lack of self confidence or experience.  Remember, there are professionals who enjoy helping young people learn.  You may have to look around to find someone like this, but they do exist.  If you focus on your goals to improve your knowledge of a particular industry, or learn better working strategies, many people will respond to that.  There are insights that only experience brings.  Once you establish a relationship, keep it alive through frequent contact.  You are being given a gift money can't buy.

# Chapter 3

# Go Beyond the Classroom

While all work and no play makes for a dull education, there are steps you can take to prepare better for the world of work.

## 1. Join a Professional Association.

Professional Associations, like the American Management Association, can be very helpful. They provide a variety of possibilities, such as:

* Opportunities to exchange ideas with others who have similar professional interests;
* Services like conferences, seminars and awards ceremonies;
* Educational materials;
* Job banks;
* Group travel and insurance benefits;
* Publication of membership directories, newsletters and magazines.

You can find one appropriate for you in the *Encyclopedia of Associations,* a reference work available in many libraries. Most national associations hold annual meetings and assist local chapters. The local chapters often meet monthly. The more established associations have college chapters which have reasonable dues and a professor who advises the organization. As soon as you can, find and join a professional association in your field, even if you are a freshman. Your college chapter may invite a professional from the business community to speak. This is a chance to network. If your association holds meetings off-campus at different businesses, they are usually well worth your time to attend. You may receive a tour of the company, you may hear a special talk on a new product or development, or meet a variety of people--whatever activities are offered--they're better than sitting in a dorm room. So many companies are difficult to visit, but by going as part of a professional organizational meeting, you're going as a guest; you may gain insights you would otherwise not have learned.

Sometimes these associations have monthly lunches, special guest speakers or an event after work.  This is your opportunity to meet working professionals in informal settings.  Try to find out about events like these, attend and keep track of who you meet.  When it comes time to look for a job, the more people you know the better off you're going to be.

## 2.  Find Internships and Get the Most From Them.

There's a consensus in colleges that internships are one of the most useful experiences for students.  They get you out of the classroom, give you real experience and allow you to meet working professionals. Internships help you determine if the career you think you want to enter is right for you.  You could hardly find a more valuable experience if it helps you do this.  Since it is that important, approach it seriously, making sure that you find an internship that will provide you with appropriate and valuable experience.  Another reason to find a good internship is that it can be a perfect place to learn.  People don't expect you to know everything, so, in a way, the pressure is off.  You can ask plenty of questions and learn as much as you can handle.  As you plan an internship, here are some important considerations.

First, internships will be valuable only if the company is willing to provide you with an appropriate experience.  Large companies with long-established programs are often adept at this.  Be careful when evaluating small companies, however.  They may not have a steady workload or a large project for you to work on.  If they do, you could have an incredible internship because fewer employees may mean you are required to perform many different jobs.  You may be given "real work," sit in on real brain-storming sessions or meetings and have the opportunity to make decisions.  The least desirable internship is one where you're main job is reading the paper or looking out the window. About any internship will look good on a resume, but you need much more than that.  Your main goals should be to acquire specific skills and the chance to observe or participate in a wide range of activities.  As you know, internships lead to jobs.  For a company, what better way to get to know you than to see you under real working conditions.  And the same is true for you.  You have the opportunity to see what it's like to work for that particular company and to meet the people who work there.  Do you feel comfortable there?  Would you fit in?  Is there a future for you?  These are the most important questions which only day-to-day experience can help you answer.

Finding a good internship may take time.  You don't know much until you look around and compare one opportunity with another.  You would be wise to investigate several internships; once you have, you'll be able to add up the advantages and disadvantages of each.  College placement offices or your advisor can probably help you identify companies.   Normally, organizations providing internships list themselves with the college.  The placement office tries to match interns to companies.  But, of course, some internships are not advertised.  If you have a special interest, talk with your advisor or major professors about it.  I also encourage you to look at some of the internship books and websites listed at the end of this section.  They may open your eyes to intriguing possibilities.

One of your best sources about internships is all around you--students who are now interns or who have already been an intern.  They can probably tell you what no one else will, so make an effort to find these people and talk to them.  You can't beat first-hand experience.  Maybe you could visit a company where a friend of yours is interning.  If not, perhaps he or she will show you the kind of work he or she's involved in.  Lastly, if you don't know anyone at a particular business, make a phone call and see if you can find a time to visit.  You probably visited the college you're attending before you enrolled.  I encourage you to treat an internship with the same caution.  You don't have to take the first one you see.   Investigate a few, then decide.   Since good internships are competitive, you may not get the one you want--a good reason to have other possibilities.  In addition, remember that everyone is busy.  It's best, therefore, to find out all you can first without taking valuable time from a manager's day.

When should you begin to look for an internship?  That depends on many factors--whether you have enough course credits and whether you feel ready.  But the earlier the better.  A junior year internship should be fully investigated in your sophomore year.  Many students are interested in particular internships and often these are located out of your region.  One of my students in Pittsburgh spent a summer with the Baltimore

Orioles and a semester also with Disney in Florida. These internships took a great deal of coordination on her part, but they were the highlight of her college career.

If you have a favorite company--whether it's American Express, General Electric, Turner Broadcasting or a smaller company, it's likely to have an internship program. If that means doing an internship out-of-town or across the country, of course, it will take more time and effort to acquire, but if it's a dream of yours to work in a certain company, the internship may turn out to be a life-altering experience. And look what it will do for your resume!   It shows that you are serious about your career, that you're willing to take risks and go the extra mile. It's what employers are looking for. It also provides an excellent starting point for a lively conversation at a job interview.

For the most current internship possibilities, it's hard to beat what the Internet offers. The following websites are worth exploring.

* One strategy that might pay off for you is to look first for companies which are hiring. Those can be found at www.careers.wsj.com. This is *The Wall Street Journal's* career site. Right now, a few on the fairly long list include Compaq, AT&T, CIGNA and GTE. Once you identify those companies that are hiring, look for internships in those same companies.

* Another possibility is to try Rising Star Internships at www.rsinternships.com. This is a comprehensive intern specialty site for students and employers. You can search, post a resume or access services which provide tips and advice on the internship experience. A random search on accounting internships nationwide turned up about 20 possibilities. More specific business categories provided fewer hits, but this shouldn't discourage you. Overall, the site could be very helpful.

* A third strategy is to browse the career centers at Netscape (http://home.netscape.com/netcenter/careercenter/)    and    Yahoo! (http://employment.yahoo.com/employment/college_central/). Both of these sites have plenty of information and services, from searches to resume help to message boards. A keyword search using, "internships in business" brought up 366 possibilities in Yahoo! They were listed in

an easy-to-follow manner. A website feature, "Internship Advice," listed 10 articles with titles like, "It's Never too Late to Find a Summer Internship," or "Turning Your Summer Internship into a Job Offer."

Below are two additional print references you may find useful:

*Internship Success: Real-World, Step-by-Step Advice on Getting the Most Out of Internships.* Marianne Ehrlich Greene. Lincolnwood, IL, VGM Career Horizons, 1998.

*Peterson's Internships 1999: More Than 50,000 Opportunities to Get an Edge in Today's Competitive Job Market.* (19th Edition). Princeton, New Jersey, Petersons Guides, 1999.

### 3.   Surf Internet Bookstores and Go to Real Ones.

Bookstores on the Internet are fabulous because they have great search engines making it easy to find what you want by title, author or key word. When you find a book you like, you will often find that it has been reviewed and rated by other readers. In addition, the bookstore will list several titles related to the book you are considering. I like to search by topic. For example, if you were interested in books on "teamwork," you could create a bibliography in a matter of minutes. Two popular bookstores on the Internet are amazon.com and barnesandnoble.com.

Real bookstores are just fun to roam through to see what you can find. You won't have the choices provided by the Internet store, but you can actually see the books you are interested in. If you go to several bookstores, you may find one which consistently has the best business or career section. A plus is that you don't have to make special trips to most bookstores. There may be one in a shopping mall where you often go. You can quickly check out the business section before you do your other shopping. Since so many book stores have great snack bars or coffee houses, you can find a few books you like and take time to review them over a cup of coffee. You may come across a wonderful selection of magazines, newspapers and sometimes music, CD ROMs and multimedia titles. Bookstores are obviously not libraries, but they can turn research and reading into a highly enjoyable experience.

## 4.  Become a Wizard at Finding Answers to Questions

The amount of information in the world continues to increase and new technologies are dramatically changing the way that it gets delivered to the end user.  The World Wide Web (WWW), electronic databases, usenet newsgroups, listservs and a number of other information distribution channels have arisen to accompany such traditional means as books and journals.  One aspect that has not changed is the need to have the skill to efficiently find that one needed piece of information.  The information explosion has complicated the information-seeking process by vastly increasing the amount of material to be searched for pertinent information and by multiplying the number of distribution channels that must be examined so as not to miss any potentially useful information.

This new information environment demands the development of skills in navigating both traditional and newly established information sources. It is a mistake to pass over print sources in the belief that the Internet contains all known information, just as it is a mistake to rely only upon books and magazine articles when electronic information resources offer fast and efficient access to much potentially useful information.  Each format and source has its own unique strengths and weaknesses.  Books and magazines will be with us for a long time to come due to certain advantages that electronic formats have not yet been able to replicate. Books have huge "bandwidth": they are the best source for a detailed analysis of a topic or wide coverage of it.  They are also comfortable to read.  Magazine articles share some of the latter attributes but are better for narrowly focused or very current information.

The new electronic media hold much more promise for supplanting magazine-type information rather than that traditionally delivered by the book.  The brief length of magazine articles (when compared to book-length treatment of a topic) and their ability to deliver reasonably current information play right to the strengths of the new information delivery technologies.  This transformation is already occurring.  The common thread that unites all information seekers is the need for *complete and effective indexing*.  No one has the time to actually read numerous copies of magazines in the hope of finding just the piece of vital information needed.  Rather, one should consult an index that covers the subject at hand and let the indexing company do your work for you.  These companies read the material, assign subject headings to it and usually provide an abstract for the content (a brief, usually one paragraph summary).  Indexes cover just about every subject area and come in a wide variety of formats.  Some are in print, some are electronic; some cover one or more entire subject area(s) while others cover one specific publication.  The first step in finding information is to find the right index for the subject that you wish to research.  There are several types of indexes.  The three main types are those that cover books, those that cover magazine articles and newspapers, and those that cover Internet resources.

Books on specific topics can be found via searches in the online catalogs of individual libraries, in multi-library catalogs and via the searchable catalogs of major book sellers.  Almost every library has an online catalog, and almost every one has access to the OCLC Worldcat database.  Worldcat is a gigantic, easily searchable database which contains nearly 40,000,000 records of works cataloged in over 30,000 libraries around the world.  If your library doesn't have a particular book, Worldcat can tell the librarian where you can find the book locally, or where you can borrow the book on Inter-Library Loan (ILL) if the libraries that own the book are not convenient.  Major booksellers have searchable online catalogs accessible via the WWW, and some like amazon.com only sell books that way- - they don't have stores.  Another way to find books is to consult the *Books in Print* database, which is great for current information as only books that are presently available from their publishers are included.

Searching for magazine and newspaper articles is getting increasingly easier.  Many indexes that used to be in print are now available electronically, which vastly expedites searching for useful information.  The latest periodical databases have integrated full text delivery capability, which means that you can sit at the PC, search the database, identify a useful article, and have the full text of the article delivered immediately to your PC without ever getting up to fetch a microfilm reel or poking through the periodical stacks.  There are several major producers of these databases and many libraries and corporations have licensed them.   Some major online libraries such as LEXIS-NEXIS have archives of periodical articles as well as wire service reports for breaking stories which support historical research as well as up-to-the minute data gathering.  *The New York Times*, *The Wall Street Journal* and other bellwether publications have enough market power to support their own index and full text delivery products.  Specialized services exist, too.  For example, *CD-Rom Professional* is the leading journal for this field. It reviews CD-Rom databases.  I particularly like the search engines provided by business magazines *Business Week, Fortune* and *Forbes*. You can easily search their archives (sometimes for a fee).  If you are in search of a subject the magazine has reported on, you can discover a gold mine of information and links to other resources.

Also, I have had good luck with the following three services when searching newspaper and journal articles.  These services are offered by many libraries.

* ProQuest Direct.  Indexing of over 3000 journals in many different fields.   The full text of over 1,600 of these journals and some newspapers is available.  More than nine years of indexing for *The New York Times* and *The Wall Street Journal* are also included.

* Business NewsBank.  The full text of more than 500 business journals and weekly newspapers are available.

* NewsBank NewsFile. Included are the full text of selected  articles from more than 500 newspapers.

There are number of other information providers.  A few of interest for business users are:

* America Online: Incredibly wide base of services, business resources and interactive sessions: 800-827-6364.

* AT&T Business Network:  About 2,500 sources:  800-660-2299.

* Compuserve:  Diverse,  traditional  business  and  consumer information services: 800-848-8990.

* IBEX:  A service of the International Business Exchange providing special services to small business, credit references and the like: 800-537-4239.

* Microsoft Network:  A multimedia news service: 800-386-5550.

* Prodigy:  News groups and special-interest data: 800-776-3449.

* PSINet:  A subsidiary of Performance Systems International.  It provides diverse international services from software exhibitions to manufacturers data and product information: 703-904- 4100.

* SBA ONLINE:  An electronic bulletin board and information resource for small businesses: 800-697-4636.

The emergence of the Internet as an information delivery vehicle has captivated the world.  Many information seekers labor under some false impressions regarding the quality and quantity of information that is on the Internet and how you find it.  The Internet does not contain all of the world's known information, and there is no guarantee that what is freely available on it is either correct or current.  There are legitimately useful sources of information on the Internet and its components-- the WWW, usenet newsgroups, and listservs--but often it is hard to find amid the clutter of digitized information.  Another consideration is that many data providers who use the Internet as a transmission vehicle for their proprietary information do not make it available to those who have not paid for the privilege.

There are search engines available for the WWW, listservs and usenet newsgroups.  Their effectiveness depends upon learning the various limiters that are unique to each search engine.  Failing to do so usually results in the retrieval of thousands of records, of which few if any will have anything to do with the topic at hand.  The search engines used for the commercial WWW databases that are subscription-only are far more sophisticated than ones such as Yahoo, HotBot and AltaVista that only search free resources.  Some large proprietary online databases with business information require the use of proprietary software for effective searches.  These include DIALOG, LEXIS-NEXIS and WESTLAW.  All of these are attempting to migrate their content to the

WWW but the transition is incomplete as of this date. These are powerful and extensive sources of information in disparate fields and no information question should ignore them if access is readily available.

One resource that is widely available and free is the advice of a reference librarian. Your local library almost always has someone who can steer you to the needed information and help you to avoid wasting time in getting it. While the librarian cannot do the research for you, he or she can tell you where the information is located, how much there is and/or what it will cost to get it.

## 5.   Start Job-Hunting Over the Internet.

In 1994, the fifteen most active online job sites posted about 15,000 jobs. By 1996, the postings had climbed to about 500,000. Now millions of jobs are listed in Internet and company web sites. But is it a good place to look for a job? It is one good strategy which you can do on your own time and at very little or no cost. You can not only look for a job, but you can also promote yourself by putting your resume in an online job bank, or even create your own website. Any of these activities could help you. Of course, they take time and skill. Putting your resume and cover letter on the Internet is becoming a common method for launching a job search. Why not? It makes it easier for people, worldwide, to find you.

To conduct a worthwhile search, you need to know typical job categories. One way to find these is to look through the job banks to see how jobs are officially categorized by the government or by companies working in a particular industry. The job category is often the first word or phrase you enter to find the type of job you want. If you don't understand the terminology used, you will not get very far. So, it would be wise to make a list of the specific job categories as you search. You can look by geographic region also. This is an excellent way to narrow your search. Some of the job banks will require that you enter information such as job title, location, specialty (hotel manager, automotive engineer, advertising account executive, etc.) and salary range. Some request that you search by date of posting and some are much easier to use than others, but all require that you follow directions specifically.  It may take longer than you expect to begin to find jobs that are appropriate for you and that interest you.

Looking for a job on the Internet is truly a learn-as-you-go process and it is essential that you're prepared for this.  By looking around online, you will find both comprehensive job banks and specialty services.  Also, many sites are helpful in unexpected ways.  They link you to other sites, so it is quite easy to move around.  Others provide educational features like bibliographies on job-searching topics or tips on improving your interviewing skills.   Others will allow you to post your resume--just follow their directions which are different for each address.  If you are worried about confidentiality, try confidential @occ.com where resumes are posted without names attached.  Electronic resumes are usually shorter than their printed equivalents.  If you plan to post your resume on line, include just your most recent and relevant experience and make the style straight-forward.  Avoid abbreviations, underlining, italics and do use the key words in your industry.  Companies are scanning resumes using computer programs, and these programs often search on the basis of key words.

Has job hunting on the Internet ever led to a job?  Yes, I know several people who have found their present jobs on the Internet.  Others have acquired leads and first interviews.   One colleague had her first interview conducted via e-mail, before she was invited to fly to the location for further interviews.

In addition to the Internet addresses listed below, you can find jobs by identifying organizations which would logically list jobs, such as: professional organizations such as the American Management Association (www.ama.org), industry trade publications such as *Advertising Age* (www.adage.com), specific organizations like Microsoft (www.microsoft.com), geographic areas like Washington, D.C. (www.dc.jobs).  Often you will see opportunities to get involved in newsgroups, a collection of discussion groups, called USENET.  They're organized by content areas.  One content area is "jobs."  You can find about 75 job-related groups through Yahoo! Click on Business and Economy on the Yahoo! Homepage.  Then you can select a city or region and enter into a discussion about jobs in a particular location.  Below you will find a list of job-related newsgroups.  There are many more and they can be also be reached through Netscape and most Internet search engines.  Don't forget, Internet addresses disappear or change.  Be flexible and keep looking.

| | |
|---|---|
| akr.jobs | Akron, Ohio jobs |
| atl.jobs | Jobs in Atlanta, GA. |
| atl.resumes | Post a resume when looking for a job in Atlanta. |
| balt.jobs | Jobs in Baltimore and Washington, D.C. |
| Co.jobs | Jobs in Colorado |
| can.jobs | Jobs in Canada. |
| chi.jobs | Jobs in the Chicago area. |
| dc.jobs | Jobs in the Washington, D.C. area. |
| Il.jobs | Jobs in Illinois |
| le.jobs | Jobs in Ireland. |
| mi.jobs | Jobs in Michigan |
| misc.jobs.misc | Job related discussion only. |
| misc.jobs.offered | For employers to post; most jobs require experience. |
| Misc.jobs.resumes | Post a job wanted message or resume. |
| e.jobs | Jobs in New England. |
| Tx.jobs | Jobs in Texas. |
| Wyo.jobs | Jobs in Wyoming |

Online job and career addresses are listed below.  Those with an asterisk would be good ones to try first.

*Adams JobBank Online: http://www.adamsonline.com
America's Employers: http://www.americasemployers.com
America's Job Bank: http://www.ajb.dni.us
Best Bets from the Net:
http://asa.ugl.lib.umich.edu/chdocs/employment/job-guide.toc.html
Boldface Jobs: http://www.boldfacejobs.com/
*Career and Life Planning Center: http://www.scs.jhu.edu/clpc/job.htm
CareerCast--http://www.careercast.com
Career Center: http://www.netline.com/career/career.html
Career Magazine: http://www.careermag.com
*CareerMosaic: http://www.careermosaic.com
CareerNET: http:www.careers.org/

*CareerPath: http//www.careerpath.com
Careers and Jobs: http://www.startthere.com/jobs/
Career Resource Center: http://www.careers.org
CareerSite: http://www.careersite.com
CareerWeb: http://www.cweb.com
Catapult: http://www.jobweb.org/catapult/catapult.htm
*College Grad Job Hunter: http://www.collegegrad.com/
CONNECT: http://www.cabrillo.cc.ca.us/connect/docs/jobs.html
CoolWorks: http://coolworks.com/showme
Corporate Staffing Center:
http://www.corporate-staffing.com/csc/hunt.html
Cruise Line Jobs: http://cruiselinejobs.com
Cybercareers: http://cybercareers,com
Epage Internet Classifieds: http://ep.com/
*Federal Jobs: http:www.fedworld.gov/jobs/jobsearch.html
Help Wanted USA: http://iccweb.com
HEART: http://www.career.com/
JobBank USA: http://www.jobbankusa.com
JobHunt: http://www.job-hunt.org
JobSmart: http://jobsmart.org
JobTrak: http://www.jobtrak.com
JobWeb: http://www.jobweb.org
*Monster Board: http://www.monster.com/
*National Association of Broadcasters: www.nab.org
NationJob Network: http://www.nationjob.com
*NetJobs Classified: http://www.ypn.com/jobs/a881.html
*OCC: Online Career Center: http://www.occ.com
Recruiters Online Network: http://www.ipa.com/
Salary Information: http://www.homefair.com
VideoPro: http://www.txdirect.net:80/videopro/default.html
Virtual Job Fair: http://www.vjf.com/
*The World Wide Web Employment Office:
http:www.harbornet.com/biz/office/annex.html
*Yahoo!Classifieds: http://classifieds.yahoo.com

## 6.  Go to Museums, Photography Exhibits, Films, Concerts and Lecture Series

Artists and musicians can be visionaries, leading society to new places. Pablo Picasso's cubist paintings took images apart and destroyed traditional visual continuity long before MTV tried similar techniques in television. Yet, I believe, there is a connection. Andy Warhol's silk screening techniques, repeated in various tones, preceded similar computer-generated graphic images.   The popularity of female musicians in the late 1990s may foresee the increased influence of women in all phases of life, including business. Only time will tell, but the important idea is to be observant and curious. Some of your best ideas and highest periods of energy may come after you have put work aside and immersed yourself in art or music.

Often it's easier to work museum visits and the like into a business or vacation trip. If you're in Washington, D.C. for a few days, visits to the Smithsonian Space Museum, the National Art Gallery or the Viet Nam Memorial will last you a lifetime. Almost all cities, even some small towns, have valuable museums and special exhibits. In the small town where I grew up, Canandaigua, N.Y., there is an incredible Native American art and history museum. Even if you have not normally found the art world to be your cup of tea, try it...you might be surprised.

When it comes to music, it seems to speak intimately and powerfully to the younger generations. Each generation seems to develop its own style. I had The Beatles and The Rolling Stones. You have your favorites. However, you might want to expand your interests. Try new types of music, new radio stations to see what else is around. When you land your first job and your boss asks you to find a variety of music for use in corporate videos, or trade shows, you will be better off if you have a broad knowledge of several music genres, appealing to a range of listeners.

Lectures sound boring to many college students. However, when you choose wisely, you can find lectures that are extremely interesting or valuable to attend. If business gurus such as Peter Drucker or Tom Peters are giving a talk at a local university, by all means go. Or, perhaps,    a    famous    architect    is    talking    about    modern architecture.  In years with major political elections, you will find plenty of speakers from which to choose.  Lectures are advertised in the same sections of newspapers as movies and concerts.  Many are free.

# Chapter 4

# Managing Communications Tools

Digital technologies are allowing us to make our communications more visual. In fact, multimedia communications which combine text, visuals and sound are becoming commonplace. This is a very recent phenomenon and it is revolutionizing communications. You can see how excited consumers are using multimedia communications. People are sending visual greeting cards over the Internet or even camcorder footage. Business is operating in the same manner because it's possible not just to create the visuals but to send them via computer modem to another location.

Multimedia communications can be clearer, more powerful and engaging--if developed and used properly. Soon, people will be surprised if you're communications are not multimedia! If you're not already, it would be worthwhile to try a few of the new technological business communications software tools to see what you like and what you can use. Avoiding their use will limit your experience and opportunities. There are training courses, but the only real way to learn to use visual communication tools is to try them.

Before we move on, one other development is worth your attention. The traditional communications software tools industries--radio, television, cable, films, books, magazines, newspapers, advertising and public relations--have already been turned upside down by digital technologies and the emergence of the Internet and world wide web. In a decade or so, will only multimedia communications firms exist to the exclusion of specialist firms like magazine publishers? For example, why should newspapers stay in the print business alone, if something better and more exciting is available? The answer is they're already moving toward multimedia communications.

* *The New York Times* on the Web provides text articles with still photographs, but it also provides audio of interviews and video segments. Furthermore, the *Times* participates in cable television

series and then it provides summaries and segments on *The New York Times* website.   Is *The New York Times* becoming an electronic publisher that includes  television?  It seems so.

* *Rolling Stone* magazine has started providing access to radio  stations through its website.

* Broadcast.com and RealNetworks (realnetworks.com) both  provide audio and video clips and news and only provide these on  the Internet. They are just two of the broadcast sources  you can find when you use an internet search engine.

* Advertising on the Internet is moving toward greater use of multimedia.  It is often more informative and more interactive than traditional advertising.

* Public relations firms make frequent use of the Internet.

* Radio stations commonly Internet cast their programming and can now add text and video.

Since all media are in the business of delivering advertising to consumers, media firms are merely finding better and more exciting ways to deliver ads using digital communications.  This trend will continue. Without knowing it, we are getting use to multimedia communications and more visual print documents.  Other less visual forms of communication are going to pale in comparison to those who use images and sound.  In business, whether it's for internal or external communications, you will find the same trends influencing your communications.  This ranges from the use of crisp, colorful charts, graphs and maps to clip art, photographs and moving pictures.  When used  with  skill,  multimedia  techniques  will  enhance  your communications.   Successful  business  communicators  will  put multimedia tools in their toolbox and use them when needed.

Below are communications technologies, software, and suggestions that you may find useful.  Some are so common, like e-mail, that they are hardly worth a mention, except that you should know the full power of the tool.  Other capabilities are evolving so when a particular software is mentioned it is only to give you a better idea of the possibilities that type of software provides. Visual communication and multimedia tools and software will only get better. I wish they'd get easier to use!

## 1.  E-mail.

E-mail is the quintessential communication to be used and not abused. Whether you're in an office, on a Navy ship, in your car or traveling internationally, e-mail has become the lifeline for business people...fast, easy, cheap and accessible most everywhere.

* Use it to its fullest.   Make sure you are up-to-speed about free Internet e-mail opportunities. Free e-mail accounts abound and many can be accessed from any computer connected to the Internet. They are extremely useful.    Some of these like Excite   Mail (www.mailexcite.com) are less cluttered with online  advertising. It also offers paging and search features which are   useful. HOTMAIL (www.hotmail.com) is very popular. It has  word processing features like a spell checker, thesaurus and dictionary so that you can edit your work efficiently. POBOX.COM (www.pobox.com) charges a yearly fee (about   $15), but it has a junk e-mail detector and an easy forwarding feature. For an additional yearly fee, you can have instant notification to your pager when important e-mail arrives. There are plenty of other e-mail services which you will find by looking around the net, talking with your colleagues or reading business and trade journals.

Features such as forwarding, sending e-mail to work groups and attaching text and multimedia documents are what puts e-mail communications in a league by itself--it is so useful only those who have spent most of their lives without it can appreciate e-mail to its fullest. The ability to connect pictures to an e-mail is revolutionary and changes communications dramatically.

* Use it appropriately. Special thank you notes are most appreciated when they arrive in letter or note card form. I'm sure expressions of thanks sent through e-mail are welcome, but they are probably forgotten as quickly as the delete key wipes them  from the screen. A card or letter demonstrates that you took special effort to say thanks.   In

addition, as wonderful as e-mail is, it can decrease face-to-face and telephone communications. Be aware of the consequences of isolating yourself. Beginning research about e-mail (and common sense) is indicating that while e-mail is easy and efficient, it is less satisfying than personal interaction.

* Maintain spelling and grammar rules in your e-mail communications. Okay, it's less formal, but don't let your guard down. Poorly written communications have less credibility. And, remember, these communications still represent you.

* E-mail is a mass communication masquerading as personal communication. And this is highly misunderstood. Personal issues that you don't want the public or your colleagues to know have no place in an e-mail. This may cramp your style, but better safe than sorry. Don't put information in an e-mail that could be embarrassing or used against you in court.

* E-mail directories can be helpful. Here are three:

* www.yahoo.com–an easy to follow and comprehensive directory.

* InfoSpace–provides personal, business, government phone, fax and e-mail.

* www.555-1212.com--provides national and international phone and e-mail directories.

## 2.  Visually Compelling--Superbly Organized Print Documents.

Business communicators should set out to create clear, visually compelling documents. In almost all cases, documents which are dense with words, organize material poorly, or are not pleasing to the eye fail to meet their goals. Proposals which cover many topics or include complex information can greatly benefit from careful attention to design, organization and presentation of the material. Gather some of the papers you have written for class. Ask yourself:

* Can you go through a paper and quickly understand its purpose?

* Can you see the main categories you were writing about?

* Are you writing about your topic in specifics, not generalities?

* Does the paper have a pleasing, professional look?

Students often place material in long paragraphs where the reader has to work hard to understand the main point, or find the separate elements of the student's argument.  This is part of the college-mind that I mentioned at the beginning of this book.  It is easier to place general statements in paragraph form and let it suffice as writing.  That won't do in the business world and no successful communicator would settle for it.  To write effectively, you not only have to know your subject well, you must be able to state your purpose simply and clearly.  You must be able to explain each separate part or category you are covering clearly, as specifically as possible and in some logical order.  And, of course, you must know your audience well so that your purpose and your material are not just clear to you, but equally clear and meaningful to your audience.  If you work hard at this, you will find that in writing about your topic, you will come to understand it better yourself.  It also means that when you have completed a document, the information is right in front of the reader to be evaluated.  Well-designed documents usually say to me that the writer understands the topic well and is writing from a position of confidence.  As you look over any of your longer papers, ask yourself if any of the following could have improved your document:

* Straight-forward table of contents;

* Executive summary of one or two pages;

* Division of main points or ideas into sections;

* Boldface titles to set off sections;

* Lists when describing three or more items, as I am doing here;

* Parallel construction so that like ideas are described in a like manner;

* Clear, concise writing using active voice.  Say what you mean.

* Strong conclusion which highlights the most persuasive or memorable points from your reader's point of view.  This is often difficult to do because you are tired of writing at this point, but remember--your conclusion is the last idea entering the reader's mind.

In regard to the look of a document:

* Be absolutely consistent in your use of font size, bolding and spacing.

* Use white space so that your pages will be pleasing to look at and easy to follow.  The white space provides relief from too many words and will help key ideas leap off the page.

* Use visuals to support your ideas or just for pizazz.  Clear, colorful charts, graphs, maps, visual models, clip art, company logos, digital photographs, key words and graphics can help you create a much more powerful communication.

* When you have the document prepared on your computer, don't just hand over the printing to someone else and not oversee it.  Take care in the printing and photocopying, using quality paper and high quality printers.  Make sure the print is dark and crisp.

Forcing yourself to write and rewrite is not easy.  It requires meticulous editing and reformatting, but it is worth it.  In addition, certain software packages can put powerful tools at your fingertips.  Microsoft Office and Lotus SmartSuite are two of these packages which provide you with a full-range of integrated tools.  These include word processing, of course, but also spreadsheets, charts, visuals such as clip art, or Internet resources.  Many other specific visual software tools are reviewed in the sections below.

## 3.   Presentation Tools.

Whether your presentations are to inform, persuade, market or sell, the skill to add visuals to your presentation can greatly enhance your impact. But there is a definite caveat here, also.   Many effective speakers use few visuals.  Visuals can reduce eye contact between you and your audience and therefore get in the way of communicating. If you do use visuals, maintain eye contact and do use your personality. Remember, Martin Luther King's "I Have a Dream" speech didn't include   one   PowerPoint   slide!   Nevertheless,   for   everyday communications certain visuals can reinforce or expand your ideas.  If you want to go beyond using traditional slides, overheads, easels or flip charts, several software packages can help you add visuals to your presentations.

PowerPoint for Windows is probably the most well known presentation software.  With it you can prepare visuals, such as titles, words on screen, add sounds, movie clips and graphics.  You can then use your presentation in a small meeting, project it for a larger audience, deliver it over the Internet, or turn it into a print document.  It's easy to use and has the features you will need.  More information on PowerPoint can be found at www.microsoft.com/

An even more powerful tool, but one with a bit higher learning curve, is Astound.  This is a stand-alone multimedia presentation package that now has the look and feel of Microsoft Office97.  You can assemble a presentation from scratch, work from over 100 templates or "headstarts," insert 3-D animation, make graphs bounce, tumble and grow.  You can create dazzling business charts with this tool.  In fact, if you are using PowerPoint, Astound could add more bang for the buck to your presentations.  It's getting easier to import audio and video clips from RealNetworks and from many other sources.  In fact, when you use video in an Astound created presentation, you have VCR-like control of the video and can fast-forward, rewind and pause the video during your talk! Of course, you can output to dynamic HTML for Web presentation without plug-ins.

An easy presentation software to use is Kai's Power Show.  This application works great with digital photos, PowerPoint slides and even video clips.  You can add video clips, TV-like text animation, sound clips and voice over narration.  You can output to a computer monitor, projector, printer and the included SHOW player.  This is a good starter tool and can help you turn dull presentations into multimedia shows. If you're interested in visual tools, look at integrated software packages like Lotus' SmartSuite, Microsoft Office or Corel Office.  Lotus Free Lance Graphics is a nifty tool in which you can quickly create visuals such as slides and add transparent GIFs.  You can import graphs and charts from other applications and create a highly professional visual presentation.

Something to remember also is that speech recognition software is available, although it needs considerable improvement.  SmartSuite uses IBM ViaVoice for Word Pro and Lotus 1-2-3 enables direct dictation into Lotus Word Pro documents and into voice-activated spreadsheet templates.  As these software tools improve, they will decrease the time you put into creating a presentation.  Speech recognition software is a major development in expanding the use of computers.  For individuals who have a learning or physical disability, speech recognition software can open up new worlds of opportunity.

## 4.  Business Graphics.

Using business graphics is more common than ever because the software packages allow you to create graphics which truly help you communicate better.  Some stand-alone graphics packages are worth considering since they give you access to thousands of images, many in 3D, listed by file names and arranged by category (nature, architecture and so on).  They allow easy use of artistic effects such as pencil sketch, inkwash, pointillism and cartoon--very nice tools.  The availability of using material from visual libraries and then editing it on your own computer make for incredible possibilities.  Two graphic packages worth considering are:  Viewpoint DataLab's LiveArt98 and TGS's LiveWork.  Both will work with Microsoft Office 97 documents such as Word and PowerPoint.  With LiveWork you can drag and drop your work into Office documents.

## 5.  Visual Libraries--Images, Clip Art, Backgrounds, Fonts and Graphics.

Savvy business communicators should know about visual libraries which supply you with royalty-free images such as logos or corporate scenes. Remember that images from books and other sources are not legally usable, unless you have secured the rights from the owners. Royalty-free libraries solve this problem and they abound.  Even if you don't have need to use visuals, the people who do more of your communication work should.  I have listed just a few of them below. More of these libraries along with their latest versions can be found in Publisher's Toolbox, 2310 Darwin Road, Madison, Wisconsin 53704-3108.  The phone number is 1-800-390-0461.

* PhotoDisc (www.photodisc.com).  This company has published on CD-ROM more than 160 discs with 336 images per disc.  The images are of high quality.  Some of the categories are: Business and Industry; Science, Technology and Medicine; Business and Transportation; Modern Technologies; Business Today; Wired Business; Global Business and Currency; and Far Eastern Business & Culture.  You can preview images online.  Discs are about $290 each.

* PhotoEssentials (www.photessentials.com).  These images feature royalty-free, model-released assignment photography.  It is ideally suited for use in advertising, brochures, reports, multimedia, websites, books and packaging.  A sampler disc is available.  The images are wonderful and often carry an emotional  quality you won't find elsewhere.

* Artville  (www.artville.com)  Artville  offers  funky,  colorful royalty-free illustrations.   Some of the categories are: Business Concepts, The World of Business, Business Relations, Working Together, International Commerce and Business Fundamentals.  The illustrations provide a highly creative, positive look.

* Logos, Trademarks, Flags and Maps.  The three volumes of these each contain over 1,000 images representing organizations, manufacturers and associations, like Coca-Cola, AT&T and AARP.  This set also includes 375 flags of countries from all over the world. There are many

atlas images and wonderful maps available. It's hard to imagine that so many images can be so easy to find and use. Try www.geoatlas.com for further information.

* The Ultimate Symbol Collection. This series includes more than 5,000 royalty-free images on three CDS; images are divided into universally recognized icons, official signs and nature icons. You can download free samples from www.ultimatesymbol.com.

* 3Tomatoes Multimedia Superpack: Graphics, photos, sounds and music for multimedia developers. This is a fairly inexpensive set of three discs combining visuals and sounds.

You can see that this is an area with a plethora of choices. Even if you are interested in historical images or fast food, you will find that there are libraries of images awaiting your use.

## 6. Internet and Video Phone.

Two prevalent trends are using the Internet for telephone calls and integrating video into the calls. These technologies have passed the experimental stage and are now fairly usable. Audio over the Internet has been improved; video still has a way to go. But nevertheless, these technologies hold promise for convenient, cheap and effective communications. They effectively collapse time and space which, of course, is their purpose. Think of a videophone as a beginning level video teleconference. The lower end systems sell for $100 or less and the software cost is nominal or even free. Most systems have a wide angle camera which sits on top of your video monitor or can be placed somewhere nearby. Some cameras swivel, a handy feature. Cameras are available in black and white, and color. If you use the Internet, as of this writing, your calls are free. Realize that while you can see and talk with several other people who also have proper setups, the quality of video is lower end; in most cases, the quality of the audio should be adequate. There are quite a few products available. One of the first was Cuseeme, an application which allows users to send and receive live video over normal phone lines. It was developed at Cornell University. I have used it and so far it has been more fun than useful, but that will change. It is a great way to stay in touch with friends, family or colleagues.  The cost is about $70.  More information is available at http://ask.simplenet.com/.

* Intel's Internet Video Phone (IIVP) has been developed as a business tool and can communicate with others who use different standards-based programs, such as Microsoft's NetMeeting.   IIVP integrates with Web directories like BigFoot and Four11, registering you so that others know you are online. Initiating calls is easy--merely follow the menu prompts--it's setting up the system that takes time and technical support. The quality of video and audio with these phone systems depends on your system and your Internet connection--so expect conditions to vary. Videophones are not for high-level meetings where extremely important matters are being decided, but for everyday communications, they are a terrific tool and will soon be a common, mainstream communication.

If you are intrigued by these systems, they're inexpensive enough to buy and find out what it takes to get it on line and how it can be used.  Even if you use it for personal reasons, it will pay off at some point in the business environment because these systems will one day be everywhere.

## 7.  Video Conferencing and Other Distance Meeting Techniques.

This is an area that is growing quickly not just because the technology is here but also because it's now less expensive.  Certain current video conferencing may still be a bit too complicated and expensive, and involve too many hassles in the setup, but they are improving in all areas. They can result in more frequent communication between distant locations and across time zones at low cost or at almost no cost.  As the user-friendliness of these systems improve, they will be a deal hard to resist.  For example, sales managers who travel extensively to meet with regional sales forces could substitute distance meeting techniques for some portion of face-to-face meetings, saving extensively on travel and living costs.  A nearby bank uses video conferencing to have loan applicants meet with a loan officer.  Many attractive opportunities like this one exist, but business communicators may want to put a toe in the water first before plunging in.  All video conferences use cameras and microphones, which capture pictures and sound, digitize and compress them and then transmit this data by computer modem, an Internet or network connection, or over an ISDN (Integrated Services Digital Network ) line.  Basic systems allow you to send and receive communications, but more sophisticated and emerging systems allow you to share data in a file, use smart boards, add titles and graphics. Like other technology, wait a few months and you will see improvement.  Costs for systems range from $800-$5,000 on up.

The basic video conference is between two people in two different locations and can be accomplished between two computer modems. Meetings with three or more locations are called multi-point meetings and are distributed over ISDN/LAN-based systems.  These systems get more expensive.

Two of the more sophisticated video conference systems on the market now are Intel's Create & Share Camera Pack PCI/Modem (www.intel.com) and Boca Video Communications Suite from Boca Research, Inc. (www.boca.com).  You need a powerful computer and fast modem to use these systems.  And, in some cases, you need patience to counter the frustration of getting the software working correctly.  But I believe these systems are extremely useful, will become common and have the potential to save companies significant amounts of money.

Other video conference systems you may want to check out are:

* ProShare Conferencing Video System 200.  This system had a very good review on the zdnet website. ( This website is excellent and provides an enormous amount of information, including reviews of communication technology and software.  I highly recommend it.  The address is: www.zdnet.com/).

* Microsoft's Net Meeting.  This application is for Windows 95+ and Windows NT.  You can hold face-to-face conversations with friends or colleagues.  It works with any video capture card or camera that supports Video for Windows.  Point-to-point or multi point conferences are possible.

If you think you will have use for these systems, start on the inexpensive end.  By the time you're ready for bigger and better systems, their prices will have probably decreased and, more importantly, their features and ease of use increased.

Another very interesting way to learn about and conduct video conferences is to look for an outside provider.  A cost-effective service is provided by Kinko's, a national chain, which as you probably know also provides desktop publishing and duplication services.  Kinko's offers PictureTel, a higher-end video conference service.  You can conduct a video conference with other Kinko's sites or at any location compatible with PictureTel.  Kinko's has video conference rooms set up to look like a typical office.  You can go point-to-point or conduct a conference with up to seven other Kinko's sites.  Setting up a video conference with Kinko's merely involves scheduling the facilities and showing up on time.  Kinko's should have a coordinator to show you how to get started and to handle any technical difficulties. Point-to-point video conferences can be conducted for a few hundred dollars.  Multipoint conferences require a site fee of about $200.  It's a hassle-free and fairly inexpensive way to conduct a video conference. It also gives you a chance to test out the viability of video conference meetings for your business. Kinko's video conference information line is 800-669-1235.  The website is www.kinkos.com/products/catalog/video.

## 8.  Digital Cameras

Next to e-mail, the digital camera will become one of the most interesting business tools of the 21st century.  Already it is small, sturdy, fairly high quality, easy to use, getting less expensive and incredibly useful for business purposes.  Of course, you can use it at the company awards banquet and post wonderful pictures on your intranet or bulletin board, but you can also use it on the production floor, in a design meeting, at the sales presentation, at a customer focus group, and on and on.  Since pictures can now be integrated into text documents, you can put these pictures in your reports and sales presentations or your talk to the Rotary Club.  Then there are the company brochures, and training materials that could benefit from visuals. You probably get the idea by now.

Digital Camcorders:  Most of what I said about digital still cameras applies to camcorders.  Of course, camcorders will give you moving pictures and sound, but if you wanted to just use freeze frames from a camcorder it almost doubles as a still camera.  Since it is getting easier to digitize video footage into a computer, and computer storage capabilities are increasing, moving pictures are going to become more and more commonplace in business communications.  The cameras are no longer expensive and soon most won't even use videotape.  A key to the use of a camcorder is to remember that moving pictures can communicate a story or sequence of events that no other medium can--the exact problem on a production line, the images and words of customers, an environmental problem, the CEO greeting at a sales meeting she couldn't attend and so on.  The possibilities are endless.

## 9.  Using and Editing Digital Images.

There are plenty of software packages to help you do this.  I have reviewed a few of these below and noted which are easier to learn.  Please remember that the software mentioned here and through out this book represent types of products--if they are not available, plenty of others will be.  In the area of still image editing, consider:

* Adobe Photoshop.  The grand daddy of them all is Adobe Photoshop which is used by creative professionals worldwide.  You can create compelling images and prepare them for distribution on the printed page, the web and about any other medium.  You can superimpose images over each other, and using virtual brushes and pens, retouch and improve any image.  The power and beauty of photoshop is that you can work in layers so that effects can be worked on separately.  This prevents a catastrophic event such as ruining an entire's day work because your various effects exist all in the same file or layer.  Photoshop's power takes time to learn and to execute.  I speak from the experience of learning the software myself, but if you have an inclination for this type of creative work, your communications can exceed the norm.

* Adobe Photo Deluxe.  This is a simpler version of photoshop, easier to learn and use.  It does not allow you to work in layers, but if speed and ease of use are important to you, this type of software is a good starting point.

* Kai's Photo Soap. Eliminates red eye, scratches, bad cropping   and faded colors.  This tool can brighten and enhance images for your presentations and print communications.  You can make calendars, greeting cards, flyers, brochures and much more.  It is made by Metacreations (www.metacreations.com). Tip:  Metacreations software is often fairly easy to learn.

* Video editing.  To use video editing software, you'll need a video capture card in your computer.  The process begins by digitizing video and sound into the video-audio capture cards in your computer.  You can quickly learn to edit your own videos by following the manuals or using CD tutorials that are often available with these products.  Of the many products available, two very good ones are Corel Lumiere Suite and Adobe Premiere.  With these applications, you can:

* Combine video, sound and still pictures;

* Add transitions, such as dissolves or special effects from a library of clips provided;

* Superimpose text or titles over pictures or backgrounds;

* Add flying logos or animations;

* Add music, sound effects and voice-over to your program;

* Convert your movie into a file that can be shown by any software application that  supports Video for    Windows   (.AVI) or QuickTime (.MOV).  The movie clips you create can be saved in various ways and then imported into your presentations, whether you plan to use them for a live presentation in a boardroom or to put them on your web page.

**10. All-Around and Drawing/Illustration Software**

* Paint Shop Pro: This is a terrific tool for business communications, digital photography and web creation. You can create, edit and manage images and interface to many other software.

* CorelDRAW. This is a high end tool for illustration, page layout, painting, photo editing, 3D modeling and rendering. It contains 40,000 clipart images and over 1000 TrueType and Type 1 fonts, plus hundreds of photos, 3D models, web backgrounds, animated GIFs, templates and more.

* FreeHand. This is a medium end tool. You can create terrific posters and brochures fairly easily with this software. A feature I especially like allows you to bind type to a curved line.

* Poster Works. This is a large-format production software. It helps you produce professional color displays, posters and billboards

**11. Web Tools and Desk Top Publishing**

The availability of web tools has skyrocketed in the last few years. Learning to use tools and applications such as HTML, JAVA or products such as Adobe PageMill, Cold Fusion Development System, Allaire HomeSite, GOLive Cyber Studio, and a variety of Microsoft products is more for the specialist. The same holds true for many desk top publishing applications like Corel Ventura. These tools are layout and design software, often with multi-user access. They allow publication to paper, Internet or portable electronic files.

**12. Management of Image Files**

Business communicators can manage visual files with several software applications. For example, Mabango Media Asset Manager organizes and searches for graphics files, fonts, transparencies and tapes. It manages both digital and physical media.

## 13. Learning to Use Visual Tools

Some people learn software on their own using the manuals supplied or by trial and error. But many other people need a structured learning environment and a knowledgeable instructor. Formal programs are available at colleges, community colleges, technical institutes, computer stores, or through traveling vendor training programs, and individual tutors. There are also many commercially available texts, CD ROMS and videos. A few are listed below.

* KW Computer Training
* VTC Training CDS
* Adobe Classroom in a Book Series
* ViaGrafix Video and CD-ROM Tutorials

You can find these in *Publisher's Toolbox* (1-800-390-0461). You could find other resources at bookstores and computer outlets or at websites: www.zdnet.com or www.pcworld.com.

## 14. Video and Audio Production

Marketing, sales, informational, and training videos remain an important and common type of business communications. They are often called nonbroadcast or industrial production, which are not very sexy terms, but billions of dollars are spent annually to communicate by large and small firms, by those in both the service and manufacturing center. Even government agencies like the Department of Commerce or the IRS produce plenty of video communications. Since they can be expensive to do, knowing how to manage a production, keep costs in line, stay on schedule are important, but not nearly as important as making sure that the video communicates the information in the manner you and your company want it communicated. And therein lies a possible quagmire. I have seen many ineffective videos because people either get lost in the complexities of this type of communication or begin to think this is their chance to be creative. Beware. Communicating through video can be extremely powerful, even highly cost effective, but get up to speed in two ways:

* Know how to select and manage an outside video production company.

* Know the process of producing a video which can be stated in three broad steps: pre-production, production and post-production.

Here is a short primer on the video production process.

* Selecting and managing a video production company: Most established companies are listed in a film and video production book which could be obtained from a local or state film bureau, from your mayor's office or local business publications.  These companies are accustomed to bidding on projects and being evaluated closely before obtaining work.  Most of these companies specialize--some do commercials, but others work closely in business communications. These are the firms that you want. Review their work by means of their company demo tape which they can send to you.  Talk with their clients. Since videos can take weeks or months to produce, it's important you develop a positive relationship with the producer.  It's also critical that the details are all on paper.  When working with one of these firms, the most important steps to take are:

* Supply the company with a clear vision of what you want to accomplish.  If a clear purpose is critical in what you write, it's even more important in a video communication.  For example, you probably will not only want certain information communicated, but also you will want to communicate a certain style so that it's motivational in tone or it makes people feel goo, and so on.

* Supply sufficient information for the scripting, but not too much. Script writers do not normally need 100 page manuals and stacks of articles.  If you overload a scriptwriter, he or she may lose focus.

* Accompany the crew on shoots or send a representative--production can be very interruptive and someone may need to handle problems.

* React quickly to scripts and material that is shot.  The 1-10-100 rule applies here.  What may cost you a dollar to fix now, could cost ten dollars next week and if you wait too long it will cost one-hundred

dollars.  If you wait to view the interviews of your executives, all the interviews may be completed before you say you don't like the way they're being shot.  If this is the case, thousands   of  dollars  can  be wasted.  Staying involved in video productions is very, very important.

All videos go through the same process of pre-production, production and post production.

* Pre-production includes the research, scripting and planning for the production.  It is common for scripts to go though several drafts. Planning for a production means knowing all the locations, people, scheduled times, special materials ahead of time.  It seems like a creative undertaking to many people, but it's really all in the details. I've seen huge three-hole binders bulging with all the planning papers. They're necessary.

* Production is the term for field and studio production--of recording what you want on tape.  This may also mean creating graphics and animation which begin by developing story boards.  Video shoots which take days are common.  The equipment is still fairly bulky, lighting is time-consuming, as is setting up and striking equipment and traveling from location to location.  A five minute interview can take an hour.

* Post production includes the editing of all your material into a professional video.  It might mean selecting a voice-over narrator, selecting or creating music, and piecing the material together into a "first cut" that usually undergoes revision until you and your colleagues are satisfied with it.

One wonderful advantage of video is that you are creating a record of the people and events in a company--it's a library of visuals available for everyone in your company to re-edit for their own purposes, such as sales presentations and speeches.  If you have captured good pictures, plenty of employees will put them to use.

# Chapter 5

# Communications Resources

You can probably find the answers to questions that you have about business communications from the resources below. For six communications specialties, I have provided professional associations, industry trade magazines and references--including directories, how-to manuals and recommended readings. Because there are so many, I have also provided an additional list of communications professional associations not included as part of those six specialities. As you can see there are many resources; however, the web pages of professional associations are emerging as comprehensive sources. They are excellent places to start your quest for further information. Please note that organizations or publications which have no website listed had none at the time of this writing.

1. Advertising and Public Relations
2. Business Communications
3. Marketing
4. Meeting Planning
5. Television/Video and Radio
6. Training and Development
7. Additional Communications Professional Associations

## 1. Advertising and Public Relations

### Professional Associations

Advertising Club of New York                 212-533-8080

American Advertising Federation              202-659-1800
                                             www.aaf.org

American Association of                       212-682-2500
Advertising Agencies                         www.aaf.org

| | |
|---|---|
| Association of Independent Commercial Producers | 212-475-2600 323-960-4763 www.aicp.com |
| Association of National Advertisers | 212-856-6300 |
| International Advertising Association | 212-557-1133 www.iaaglobal.org |
| Public Relations Society of America | 212-995-2230 www.prsa.org |
| Radio Advertising Bureau | 212-681-7200 www.rab.com |

## Industry Trade Magazines

| | |
|---|---|
| *Advertising Age* | 212-210-0100 www.adage.com |
| *Advertising Age International* | 212-210-0100 www.adage.com |
| *Advertising Communications Times* | 215-629-1666 |
| *American Advertising* | 202-898-0089 www.aaf.org |
| *Tactics (Monthly Newspaper)* | 212-995-2230 www.prsa.org |

## References:

*Standard Directory of Advertisers.* National Register Publishing Co., Skokie, IL. This is the most comprehensive directory of advertising agencies.

*The Complete Advertising and Marketing Handbook.*  Hershell Gordon Lewis, Bonus Books, Chicago, 1998.

*Career Opportunities in Advertising and Public Relations.*  Shelly Field (editor), Facts on File, New York, 1996.

*O Dwyer's Directory of PR Firms.* J. R. O'Dwyer Incorporated, Bowker, 1998.

*Lesly's Handbook of Public Relations and Communications (5th edition).* Contemporary Books, Lincolnwood, IL, 1998.

*Public Relations Handbook.* IABC: available at www.iabc.com.

## 2.  Business Communications

### Professional Organizations

| | |
|---|---|
| Association for Business Communication | 212-387-1340 |
| International Association of Business Communicators | 415-433-3400 www.iabc.com |

### Industry Trade Magazine

| | |
|---|---|
| *Communication World* | 415-433-3400 www.iabc.com |

### References

| | |
|---|---|
| *Business Information Sources* | 510-642-4247 |

*Corporate Communications for Executives.*  Michael B. Goodman, State University of New York Press, Albany, NY, 1998.  This work covers communication in management, corporate public relations, social responsibility of business, corporate culture and communication in organizations.

*Crisis Management & Communication: How to Gain and Maintain Control.* Robert B. Levine and Dan P. Millar, Ph.D., IABC, www.iabc.com.

*Effective Media Relations: A Practical Guide for Communicators.* Wilma K. Mathews, ABC, IABC, www.iabc.com.

*Global Business Communication: Adopting a World View.* Norman G. Leaper, ABC, IABC, www.iabc.com.

*The New York Public Library Business Desk Reference: Essential Information for Every Office--at Your Fingertips.* Paul Fargis and Sheree Bykofsky, Editorial Directors, New York, John Wiley & Sons, 1998.

## 3.  Marketing

### Professional Associations

| | |
|---|---|
| American Marketing Association | 312-648-0536 |
| | 800-262-1150 |
| | www.ama.org |
| Business Marketing Association | 800-664-4262 |
| | www.marketing.org |
| Promotion Marketing Association of America | 212-420-1100 |
| Sales and Marketing Executives International | 216-771-6650 |
| | www.salesand marketing.com |

### Industry Trade Magazines

| | |
|---|---|
| *Business Marketing* | 312-649-5260 |
| *Marketing News* | 312-648-0536 |
| *Sales & Marketing Management* | 800-821-6897 |
| | www.salesand marketing.com |

## References

*American Marketing Association International Member & Marketing Services Guide.* American Marketing Association, Chicago, 1998.

*American Marketing Association Yellow Pages & International Membership Directory.* American Marketing Association, Chicago, 1998.

*Business to Business Marketing.* Victor L. Hunter and David Tietyin, Lincolnwood, IL, NTC Business Books, 1997.

*Creating & Delivering Winning Advertising & Marketing Presentations.* Sandra Moriarty, Tom Duncan and Anee Knudsen (editor). Lincolnwood, IL, NTC Business Books, 1995.

*Managing Business to Business Marketing Communications.* Nicholas J. De Bonis,  Roger S. Peterson and Joe Vitale, Lincolnwood, IL, NTC Business Books, 1997.

*Marketing Essentials.* Lois Farese,  Glencoe/McGraw-Hill, New York, 1997.

*Marketing for Dummie.*  Alexander Hiam, IDG Books, Foster City, CA, 1997.

*Principles of Marketing.* Phillip Kotler and Gray Armstrong, Prentice-Hall, 1998.

## 4.  Meeting Planning

### Professional Associations

| | |
|---|---|
| International Association for Exposition Management | 972-458-8002 |
| | www.iaem.org |
| Connected International Meeting Professionals | 703-978-6287 |
| (International Institute of Convention Management) | www.cicm.com |

## Trade Magazine

*Presenting Communications*                                913-469-1110

## References

*Directory of Association Meeting Planners & Conference Convention Directors 1998.* Salesman Guide Staff, 1998.

*Planning Successful Meetings and Events.* Ann J. Boehme, AMACOM, New York, 1998.

*The Complete Guide to Special Event Management.* Wiley, New York, 1992. Provides business insights, financial advice, and successful strategies from Ernst & Young--consultants to the Olympics, the Emmy Awards and the PGA Tour.

*How To Organize a Conference.* Iain Maitland, Gower, Brookfield, VT, 1996.

## 5.  Television/Video/Radio

## Professional Associations

National Association of Broadcasters                        202-429-5300
                                                           www.nab.org

National Cable Television Association                       202-775-3550
                                                           www.ncta.com

International Television and Video Association              972-869-1112
                                                           www.itva.org

International Radio and Television Society Foundation   212-867-6650
                                                           www.irts.org

## Industry Trade Magazines

| | |
|---|---|
| *A/V Video & Multimedia Producer* | 914-328-9157 |
| | www.avvideo.com |
| | |
| *Broadcasting & Cable* | 212-337-6940 |
| | www.broadcastingandcable.com |
| | |
| *Hollywood Reporter* | www.hollywoodreporter.com |
| | |
| *Shoot* | 212-764-7300 |
| | |
| *Variety* | 212-645-0067 |
| | 323-857-6600 |
| | www.variety.com |
| | |
| *Videography* | 212-378-0400 |
| | www.videography.com |
| | |
| *Video Systems* | 800-441-0294 |
| | www.videosystems.com |

## Resources and References

Radio Advertising Bureau (www.rab.com):  a wonderful source for radio and media information.  The site includes statistics regarding audiences, listener profiles and RAB's Radio Marketing Guide & Fact Book.

Television Bureau of Advertising (www.adweb.com):  This is a very thorough site providing a wide range of statistics and useful information about television households, VCR households and time spent viewing. It also discusses television trends and has a glossary of television terms.

*Bacon's Directories*.  Bacon's Radio/TV/Cable Directory is an annual directory.  It lists media contact information for U.S. radio and TV stations.

*BIB Television Programming Sourcebooks.* This is a four-volume reference on syndicated programming.

*Bowker's Complete Video Directory.* This reference includes a wealth of information. It also has a yellow pages, providing addresses, phone numbers and key names within each organization. It's valuable because of its comprehensive and specific information.

*Broadcasting & Cable Yearbook.* This is a comprehensive resource providing insight into key developments and trends in the field. It is also includes lists and contacts for all radio and TV stations in the U.S. In addition, it has sections on government agencies and ownership; equipment suppliers and services; programming suppliers; trade associations, events education and awards; *Trade Show Week Data Book*; media related books, periodicals and videos; It is published by R.R. Bowker.

*Broadcast Interview Source.* This is a guide to thousands of experts and sources, along with addresses and phone numbers. Information can be searched by topic, by state, or organization name.

*Communications Industry Forecast.* This provides short and long-term forecasts based on extensive historical data. *Communications Industry Report* examines communications industry public company performance information. Financials are reported by company and by industry segment. It covers media businesses in the United States, Canada, and Mexico.

*R&R Program Supplier Guide.* This is more than a guide. It includes listings of syndicated programs, radio networks, satellite formats, production music libraries, jingle packages and much more.

*Television & Cable Factbook.* This is a directory of television stations and cable systems covering everything from the markets each serves to the types of equipment each station uses and the people employed.

*TBI (Television Business International) Yearbook.*  Provides information on the television industry worldwide, including satellite, cable TV, regulatory organizations and trade associations.

*TV Dimensions.*  It offers comparative ratings information, the impact of cable, out-of-home viewing, program mortality rates, demographic profiles, dial switching, commercial exposure, commercial impact, competitive clutter, TV sales effects, advertising on the Internet and much more.  Published by Media Dynamics, Inc,

*World Guide to Television.*  It provides addresses and phone numbers for television decision-makers in 185 countries.  It also includes a very thorough section on station formats, coverage areas, data on cable and satellite companies and television distributors.

## Media Research

*BIA Research Inc's Radio Yearbook and BIA's Television Yearbook.*  They highlight more than 10,000 radio stations and over 1,600 television stations stressing market performance of each station and key employees.  Both ratings information and technical data are included.  Plus there are helpful lists of broadcast industry related vendors and service providers.

*BIA Research Inc.'s State of the Radio Industry and BIA's State of the Television Industry.*  They provide current status and trends analysis.

## 6.  Training and Development

### Professional Organization

American Society for Training and Development      703-683-8100
                                                  www.astd.org/

### Industry Trade Magazines

*Training & Development*                          www.astd.org/

*Technical Training Magazine*                     www.astd.org/

## References

*Effective Training: Systems, Strategies, and Practices*. Nick P. Blanchard, Prentice Hall, Englewood Cliffs, NJ, 1999.

*How To Be an Effective Trainer: Skills for Managers and New Trainers*. Brian L. Delahaye, John Wiley, New York, 1998.

*The Trainer's Handbook*: *The AMA Guide to Effective Training*. AMACOM, New York, 1998.

## 7.  Additional Communications Professional Associations

| | |
|---|---|
| American News Women's Club | 202-332-6770 |
| American Society of Journalists and Authors | 212-997-0947 |
| American Society of Magazine Editors | 212-872-3700 |
| American Sportscasters Association (ASA) | 212-227-8080 |
| American Women in Radio and Television | 703-506-3290 |
| Black Women in Publishing | 212-427-8100 |
| International Interactive Communications Society | 503-579-4427 |
| Internet Society | 703-648-9888 |
| | 800-468-9507 |
| Magazine Publishers of America (MPA) | 212-872-3700 |
| National Academy of Television Arts and Sciences | 212-586-8424 |
| National Association of Media Women (NAME) | 404-344-5862 |
| National Association of Minority Media Executives | 703-709-5245 |

National Association of Television Programming          310-453-4440
Executives (NATPE)

Video Software Dealers Association                      818-385-1500

Vidion/International Association of Video
Game Players                                           202-328-9276

## Conclusion

Becoming the communicator you want to be is not going to happen over
a semester and probably not over your college career.  But if you take
your business course work in earnest, absorb a few ideas from here and
begin to read and widen your interests, then you're on a good path.  A
personal mission statement is a good place to start along with a
subscription to *The Wall Street Journal*.  Best wishes as you navigate
the exciting and often turbulent waters of a business career.

## CHAPTER NOTES

### Chapter 1

1. Collins, James C. And Jerry I. Porras. *Built to Last: Successful Habits of Visionary Companies*, (New York: Harper Collins Publishers, 1994), 82.

2. "Values Statement," Merck Website (1 Jan. 1999): Retrieved Feb. 15, 1999 from the World Wide Web: http://www.merck.com. Copyright Merck & Co., Inc., Whitehouse Station, N.J., U.S.A. All Rights Reserved. Reprinted with permission of Merck & Co., Inc.

3. "Our Values," General Electric Website (1 Jan. 1999): Retrieved Mar. 20, 1999 from the World Wide Web: http://ge.com. Reprinted with permission of General Electric.

4. Morita, Akio with Edwin M. Reingold and Mitsuko Shimomura. *Akio Morita and Sony*, (New York: E.P. Dutton, 1986), 147. Reprinted with permission of Penguin Putnam Inc.

5. *Bartlett's Familiar Quotations*, Fifteenth Edition, 686.

6. Walton, Sam with John *Huey. Sam Walton: Made in America,* (New York: Doubleday, 1992), 249. Reprinted with permission of Doubleday.

7. Collins and Porras, *Built to Last*, 9.

8. "Special Message to Congress on Urgent National Needs," (Public Papers of the President, May 25, 1961), 404.

9. Kelley, Robert E. *How to be a Star at Work: Nine Breakthrough Strategies You Need to Exceed*, (New York: Random House, 1998), 42.

10. "Apollo 13." Director, Ron Howard. With Tom Hanks, Fred Haise and Jack Swigert, Universal Pictures, 1995.

11. Raeburn, Paul. *Mars: Uncovering the Secrets of the Red Planet*, (Washington, D.C.: National Geographic Society, 1998).

12. Collins and Porras, *Built to Last*, 43.

13. Dewey, John. *How We Think*, (1950; reprint, Buffalo: Prometheus Books, 1991), 72.

14. Bales, Robert. *Interaction Process Analysis: A Method for the Study of Small Groups*, (1950; reprint, Chicago, University of Chicago Press, 1976).

15. Briggs Myers, Isabel with Peter B. Myers. *Gifts Differing*, (Palo Alto: Consulting Psychologists Press, Inc., 1980), 1.

16. Lewis, James P. *The Project Manager's Desk Reference: A Comprehensive Guide to Project Planning, Scheduling, Evaluation, Control & Systems*, (Chicago: Irwin Professional Publishing, 1995), 345-370. Reprinted with permission of The McGraw-Hill Companies.

17. Kelley, *How to be a Star*, 184-200.

18. Lewis, *The Project Manager's Desk Reference*, 360.

19. Adapted from *The Team Handbook Second Edition*. Copyright 1996 Oriel Incorporated. All Rights Reserved. Scholtes, Peter R., Brian L. Joiner and Barbara J. Streibel. Oriel Incorporated, Madison, Wisconsin: Oriel, 6-4--6-7. Used with permission.

20. Covey, Stephen R. *The Seven Habits of Highly Effective People: Powerful Lessons in Change*, (New York: Simon & Shuster, 1989), 78.

21.  Janis, Irving. *Groupthink: Psychological Studies of Policy Decisions and Fiascoes*, 2nd ed.  (Boston: Houghton Mifflin Company, 1982).

22.  Schlesinger, Jr., Arthur M.  *A Thousand Days: John F. Kennedy in the White House*, (Boston: Houghton Mifflin Company, 1965), 233-297.

23.  Vaughn, Diane.  *The Challenger Launch Decision: Risky Technology, Culture, and NASA*, (Chicago: University of Chicago Press, 1996).  This is one of several good books on the subject.

24.  Brandenburger, Adam M. and Barry J. Nalebuff.  *Co-opetition,* (New York: Doubleday Currency, 1996), 1.

25.  "U.S. Equal Employment Opportunity Commission National Enforcement Plan," Equal Employment Opportunity Commission Website (7 Mar. 1998): Retrieved Mar. 28, 1999 from the World Wide Web: http://www.eeoc.gov.

26.  "Diverse Top Management Boosts Bottom Line," American Management Association Website (Mar. 1999): Retrieved Mar. 25, 1999 from the World Wide Web: http://www.amanet.org/research/press/html.

27.  "Section 703 (a) (1) of Title VII of the Civil Rights Act of 1964," Equal Employment Opportunity Commission Website: Retrieved Jan. 15, 1999 from the World Wide Web: http://www.eeoc.gov.

28.  "Federal Laws Prohibiting Job Discrimination: Questions and Answers," (Washington, D.C.: United States, GPO, 1998), 7.

29.  "Facts About Age Discrimination," (Washington, D.C.: United States, Equal Employment Opportunity Commission, GPO, 1996).

30.  "Facts About the Americans with Disabilities Act," (Washington, D.C.: United States, Equal Employment Opportunity Commission, GPO, 1998).

31.  "Federal Laws Prohibiting Job Discrimination," 10.

32.  "Facts About Pregnancy Discrimination, (Washington, D.C.: United States, Equal Employment Opportunity Commission, GPO, 1998).

33.  "Federal Laws Prohibiting Job Discrimination," 2-3.

34.  "Facts About Sexual Harassment," (1998) and "Questions and Answers About Sexual Harassment: Identifying Sexual Harassment," (1995) (Washington, D.C.: United States, Equal Opportunity Employment Commission, GPO).

35.  "The Four-Way Test of What We Think, Say, or Do," Rotary International Website: (1932) Retrieved Feb. 20, 1999 from the World Wide Web: http://www.rotary.org/whatis/part_II.html#4way. Reprinted with permission of Rotary International.

36.  Blanchard, Kenneth and Norman Vincent Peale. *The Power of Ethical Management*, (New York: William Morrow and Company, 1988) 20-24.

37.  Ibid., 69.

38.  "Our Credo," Johnson and Johnson Website (1999): Retrieved Mar. 20, 1999 from the World Wide Web: http://www.johnsonandjohnson.com. Reprinted with permission of Johnson & Johnson Company.

## CHAPTER 2

1.  Debono, Edward. *Lateral Thinking: Creativity Step-by-Step*, (New York: Harper Collins Publishers, 1990).

2.  Drucker, Peter, "The Next Information Revolution," *ASAP, Forbes Digital Tool* (8.24.98): Retrieved Oct. 10, 1998 from the World Wide Web: http://www.forbes.com.

3.  *Kelley, How to be a Star*, 64-87.